By Grace Transformed

By Grace Transformed

Christianity for a New Millennium

N. Gordon Cosby

A Crossroad Book
The Crossroad Publishing Company
New York

The Crossroad Publishing Company
370 Lexington Avenue, New York, New York 10017

Printed in the United States of America

Unless otherwise noted, scripture is quoted from the *New English Bible*.

The Author and Publisher wish to thank the following for permission to reprint excerpts from previously published material:
Morale by John W. Gardner, Copyright ©1978 by John W. Gardner. Reprinted by permission of W.W. Norton & Co., Inc: New York. **The Coming of the Cosmic Christ** by Matthew Fox. Copyright © 1988 Matthew Fox. Reprinted by permission of HarperCollins Publishers Inc. **The Kingdom Within: The Inner Meanings of Jesus' Sayings**, revised edition by John A. Sanford. Copyright © 1987 by John A. Sanford. Reprinted by permission of HarperCollins Publishers Inc. **Dreams: God's Forgotten Language** by John Sanford. Copyright © 1968 by John Sanford. Reprinted by permission of HarperCollins Publishers Inc. **Creative Prayer** by Emily Herman (Harper & Brothers: New York and London, 1934). Reprinted by permission of Sun Publishing Company, Sante Fe, New Mexico. **Letters to Marc about Jesus** by Henri J. M. Nouwen. Copyright © 1987, 1988 by Henri J. M. Nouwen. English translation copyright © 1988 by Harper & Row, Publishers, Inc. and Darton, Longman & Todd, Ltd. Reprinted by permission of HarperCollins Publishers Inc. **Shalom** by Ulrich Duchrow and Gerhard Liedke, Geneva, 1989. Reprinted by permission of WCC Publications. Thomas Merton: **New Seeds of Contemplation**. Copyright © 1972 by The Abbey of Gethsemani, Inc. Reprinted by permission of New Directions Pub. Corp. Every effort to reach copyright holders has been made. We will be glad to publish additional credits in future printings with proper notification.

Library of Congress Cataloging-in-Publication Data

Cosby, N. Gordon.
  By grace transformed : Christianity for a new millennium / by N.
Gordon Cosby.
      p. cm.
  Includes bibliographical references (p.).
  ISBN 0-8245-1754-7 (pbk.)
    1. Christian leadership—Sermons. 2. Sermons, American,
3. Christian life—Sermons. 4 Mission of the church—Sermons.
5. Church of the Saviour (Washington, D.C.) 6. Cosby, N. Gordon.
I. Title.
BV652.1.C68 1998
252—dc21   98-6084
                                                                  CIP

    1   2   3   4   5   6   7   8   9   10   03   02   01   00   99

To the memory of
Julian Nichols
(1934–1998),
a life transformed
by grace.

Contents

Foreword   ix

Introduction   xiii

PART I
STARTING POINT

1   This I Have Learned   3

PART II
A NEW KIND OF LEADERSHIP

2   The Nature of Christian Leadership   13

3   Servant Leadership   23

4   The Ministry and the Ministries   33

PART III
LIVING TOGETHER IN CHRIST

5   The Way to Life   43

6   Oneness   51

7   Discipline of Love   60

8   Forgiveness—A Start   69

9   Forgiveness—A Continuing Experience   76

10   Intercessory Prayer   86

**PART IV
AFFIRMING GIFTS**

11 Calling Forth Gifts   95

12 Called to Be Prophets   106

13 Called to Be Creative   115

**PART V
OVERCOMING FEAR**

14 God's Answer for Anxiety   127

15 Reducing Fear   134

16 Detachment   145

**PART VI
EXPANDING VISION, REACHING OUT**

17 Deepening Connections   155

18 Pain, Power, and the Poor   165

19 March for Freedom in Selma   175

20 Crusade for Captive Children   184

21 How Much Is Enough?   192

**PART VII
OLD BATTLES, NEW CHALLENGES**

22 D-Day—Then and Now   205

Foreword

A book of sermons! Why would anyone want to read another one of those? Well, of course, a great sermon is really an art form, and a great preacher can fill the listener with as much feeling and inspiration as can a great musician, actor, or poet. And Gordon Cosby is truly a great preacher. In his resonant Virginia drawl, Cosby combines a lively biblical imagination with the passion of an Old Testament prophet *and* the nurturing spirit of a seasoned spiritual guide—a rare blend indeed. Listen to the eighty-year-old Gordon Cosby and what you hear is wisdom—a characteristic in short supply these days. But none of these is reason enough to read another book of sermons. The reason is much deeper.

You see, for all the talk in both the religious and political world today about "the churches," there is amazingly little attention given to the phenomenon of a group of people trying to live together in the world according to the way that Jesus taught. It is simply astounding how many respected church leaders, renowned theologians, famed television evangelists, and most certainly, those moral guardians of society seeking to forge the faithful into an intimidating political power bloc, have simply bypassed the question of the "local church."

What actually is this thing called church supposed to look like, act like, and be like in the lives of ordinary people and ordinary communities? It is such a basic and foundational question and perhaps that's why it has been so widely avoided. But that question—the meaning and shape of the local church—has occupied Gordon Cosby for most of his eighty years.

He started thinking and talking about these questions with his teenage sweetheart, Mary, who later became his wife and co-founder of The Church of the Saviour—where *all* these sermons have been preached.

Unlike most great preachers, Gordon Cosby never had a career in the traditional sense. As a wartime chaplain in Europe, young Cosby made the startling observation that Christian faith really didn't mean very much to the way American soldiers lived or died.

Determined that faith must mean something more, he came home to start a new church and has never left it. Because Gordon and Mary's early vision was so exciting, many thought (including them for a time) that the possibilities for growth were enormous. There was even some interest from a Rockefeller in funding The Church of the Saviour. But the "spiritual disciplines" proved too daunting for most.

After thirty years, The Church of the Saviour had fewer than two hundred members in 1976. But the membership decided the church was getting too large and divided themselves into a number of related faith communities. Today, the twelve faith communities that have grown out of The Church of the Saviour together number about two hundred and fifty people—not so impressive in this era of mega-churches.

What Gordon Cosby imparts in this extraordinary book of sermons is a vision for the local church honed in the crucible of more than five decades of experimenting with the Gospel. It is a far more practical and powerful vision of the body of Christ than one can find almost any-where else. Perhaps Gordon Cosby's vision is so radical because it dares to ask and wrestle with the most basic questions.

First, these sermons show the heart of a pastor who actually believes that the church should be defined by *commitment*. Imagine that! These days churches are so desperate to find new members that they will take anybody on almost any basis. In contrast, The Church of the Saviour actually makes it difficult to join because of all it asks of its members.

Yet in reading Gordon Cosby's sermons your spirit begins to rise to the call of discipleship that set fire to the earliest communities of Christian believers.

These sermons also literally ring with the call to *mission*. This preacher is utterly convinced that following Jesus means to offer your life and your gifts for the sake of the world, and especially for the poor. That conviction has proven as simple as it is powerful. Out of The Church of the Saviour these have grown: countless housing units and jobs for poor families; programs for inner-city youth; health care for the homeless and immigrants; havens and healing for the addicted, the aged and the dying; and, perhaps most of all, hope for all those who would otherwise have just given up.

The Church of the Saviour has "called" into being literally hundreds of ministries, raised millions of dollars, and touched the lives of tens of thousands of people. At any given time their faith communities are likely to have more ministries than they have members, often drawing in hundreds of others who want to help them serve. Now how do you explain how a little church creates more ministry than any mega-church or even group of them in the whole rest of the country? Read these sermons to find out.

But ultimately, Gordon Cosby's sermons call us to a quality of *being* in the Christian life even more deeply than to a life of *doing*. For more than fifty years the people of The Church of the Saviour have been learning how to pray. Without the spiritual center, Gordon Cosby has preached, all of our activity can easily become fruitless and even destructive.

In "listening" to the sermons printed here, one hears the voice of a wise spiritual director guiding each of us through a contemplative retreat in the countryside. It is the *essence* of The Church of the Saviour that the founding pastor wants to pass on to a new generation, more than a collection of ministries.

In these sermons of Gordon Cosby you will find an evangelist still struggling with the question of how truly to live out the Gospel. Over a recent lunch conversation the voice of experience does not revel in successes but rather worries about the state of the church, even his own.

"We've done a lot of work with addicts," he says, "and we've learned that what they really need is a drug-free community environment in order to be healed. . . . I'm afraid the churches are just enabling the addictions of our culture. If we are not free from the cultural addictions in the church, how can we be a healing presence for all those who need to be set free?"

That's Gordon Cosby. Always asking the most basic Gospel questions. And that's why you should read this unique and extraordinary book of sermons.

—JIM WALLIS
Publisher, *Sojourners*

Introduction

Gordon Cosby returned from duty as a chaplain in the 101st Airborne Division during World War II with a vision of church that had been forged in the chaos and trauma of the invasion of Normandy and the subsequent fierce fighting in France. Gordon's vision of the Gospel message was a challenge to the conventional consciousness of the time.

Gordon had concluded that a church that is faithful to the Gospel message requires an interracial congregation that is well grounded in the essentials of the Christian faith and committed to and accountable for inner growth, active participation in mission, and proportionate giving.

A small group of people responded with an enthusiasm for this concept of church that mirrored Gordon's enthusiasm, and on October 5, 1946, the first meeting of The Church of the Saviour was held with nine people attending.

Over a fifty-year period, The Church of the Saviour has evolved and grown, separating in 1976 into separate loosely connected faith communities. Finally, in 1994, nearly fifty years after the founding of The Church of the Saviour, the twelve faith communities it spawned became separately incorporated. Thus, The Church of the Saviour, which began with nine members, has been transformed into twelve small churches with a common heritage.

Elizabeth O'Connor has beautifully recounted the early days of The Church of the Saviour in her books, but much of the story of the latter half of its life remains to be told. It is the story of a small community, faithful in prayer and open to challenge, growing in understanding and commitment to the guidance of the Holy Spirit, being confronted with increasingly greater opportunity and greater challenge.

During the fifty-year period of the life of The Church of the Saviour, the church has been nurtured, challenged, and moved to action by the prophetic nature of the sermons of Gordon Cosby. Of course, Gordon has done much more than preach from the pulpit. He has taught, counseled, encouraged, and consoled, and his creative mind has continually churned out new ideas and new challenges. His attention and presence have been lavished on his small flock. But it has been his sermons that have called into being and have sustained The Church of the Saviour and its many major missions.

Along the way Gordon has been given many invitations to speak to groups of Christians and to preach in different parts of the country. However, Gordon has placed his highest priority on being present and active in the work of the community that he considers entrusted to him by Christ. After a few years he refused all invitations to travel and speak to groups around the country, devoting himself to calling forth and nurturing new missions and delivering his sermons to a congregation that has been small by almost any standard. It is perhaps one of the reasons why these sermons have a freshness and relevance that transcend the location and time in which they were first delivered.

—JULIAN NICHOLS

Member, The Church of the Saviour

Part I

~∾~

Starting Point

1

This I Have Learned

~

In 1956, ten years after the first meeting of the small group of people who became The Church of the Saviour, Gordon was given the opportunity to reflect on how this church came into existence and the lessons that were learned in its first decade.

Some months ago Elton Trueblood invited me to speak to a convocation of several hundred ministers at Earlham College in Richmond, Indiana, on the topic, "How The Church of the Saviour came into existence, and what I have learned over the intervening period of nine years with the church." And he told me to say it all in thirty minutes!

As I reflected on that topic, I realized my experience in England and on the continent of Europe during World War II had brought into focus certain thoughts and convictions which I had held for many years.

One incident I recall took place in England. One night a young man came into my chaplain's office. He was from the same company as that of a man whom I had recently baptized. I asked, "How is so-and-so getting along in his Christian life?" He asked me what I meant, and I said, "Just what I said, how is so-and-so getting along in his Christian life?" He replied, "I don't know what you mean." So I said to him, "Well, just a week or so ago, after several conferences with him concerning the meaning of the Christian life, I baptized him. I would like to know what progress he is making, what sort of witness he is making in his company."

This young man, a faithful Christian and a good friend, put his head back and started laughing. He said, "If old so-and-so is a Christian, no one in the company knows it!"

Something snapped within my soul that night, and I began to ask myself the question, "What am I doing? If I'm having conferences with

3

these men, if I am baptizing them into the Christian faith and the
people in the company cannot tell the difference, what am I doing?"

Up until this time I had been doing what most chaplains do. I had
been sending in a favorable report every month concerning the number
of conversions which had occurred under my ministry. Until that time I
had had some fifty, seventy-five, or one hundred every month. Now
these numbers were genuine; these were people who had responded to
an invitation. I had baptized these people. I was happy to send in such a
report, because a chaplain's status is somewhat determined by his
number of conversions. If everyone else was reporting fifty, seventy-five,
or one hundred, and you were reporting fewer, that was not so good.

As I thought about this, I realized that I was in a situation which did
not take much spiritual courage to change. I was a first lieutenant, and
you can't be a chaplain if you are lower in rank than a first lieutenant,
so they couldn't demote me. The only thing they could do would be to
send me back to the States, and since this was a week or two before
Normandy, nothing under those circumstances would have suited me
better! So I said, "What have I to lose if from now on I report two
conversions, if I report five, if I report none? From now on I am going
to be *real* in my ministry. I will work for a lifetime, if need be, with one
person, with five persons, with ten. The Christian faith should make a
difference in the life of a person, and this will be my kind of ministry."

Another situation into which I was thrown was helpful. Day after day
I stood before groups of men—twenty, thirty, forty—who gathered in
the snow of a bitter winter at the risk of their lives to worship for ten or
fifteen minutes before going into battle. For many of them it was going
to be their last battle. I stood in the snow with those men and talked
with them out of the depths of my heart. I preached five-minute
sermons. I stood there when it was so cold I could not make my mouth
move to finish the benediction. I came to know that, under those
circumstances, I had to have something more real, more valid, to say
than I had been saying before, because I was talking to some men for the
last time. They would be reporting to the God before whom I had taken
my vows for the ministry. I knew I had to have a ministry which was real.

When I came back to Washington I had one thing in mind, as did
others who have shared in the dream ever since. We wanted to give
God an opportunity to see what would happen in a community of
committed people. This would not be a community which is withdrawn,
and which pulls out of society as we know it, but it would be a community that lives among people. The commitment of our lives would be so

deep and our bond would be so real that the Holy Spirit would have opportunity to create a community of faith. From this would come a belonging that would be something different, something God could use in a marvelous way for the extension of the kingdom.

Now what have I learned in a period of nine years of ministry?

The first thing I have discovered is that an encounter with the living Christ is a much more radical experience than I had conceived it to be nine years ago. I have found that it takes time for people to see what the issues are. People come and touch the life of our fellowship, and they feel that the fellowship is the significant thing. They come to know the joy of creative work, of belonging to something which is meaningful, and they feel the creative work is the significant thing. Then one day they draw closer and closer to the heart of this church, and they find that they must have a personal encounter with the living God. This is the frightening thing—something that makes them withdraw, for they know it to be irrevocable. It is something for time and eternity. Once allegiance has been given to Christ there can be no drawing back. Some people leave temporarily and, years later, return because they had tasted a quality of experience which they realize they must have. As they had grown close to the One who is the very heart of our life together, they found this to be a more radical and profound experience than they had had any idea that it would be.

The second thing I have discovered is that commitment and discipline are the absolute essentials of any spiritual power. I do not mean a general commitment or general discipline. I mean a definite commitment to the Lord Jesus Christ. This is a commitment to a person—not a commitment to a cause. Not commitment to a principle of love, this is commitment to a living person, and it is definite.

Not only must it be definite, but it must be a full commitment. When Christ comes to a person he makes a total claim upon his or her life; only a total response is adequate. Not to respond in such a definite way is not to have met the real Christ. If Christ is not a figment of our imagination, we make a commitment in which we can say with freedom of spirit: "I belong solely to him. He is my life. He is the hope of every dream. He is of absolute significance to me. I want you to know him." Such a commitment is the essential of any sort of Christian power.

Along with this there must be specific discipline. A general discipline is no good; it must be specific. It must relate itself to the world of persons. We must commit ourselves to loving people. If not, there will be times of pressure when we will not love them. We need specific discipline at the point of money. We need specific discipline at the point of the total material universe. Otherwise, there will be times when we will not relate properly. The material world will control us, rather than our being its master with Christ. We need specific discipline at the point of time. If we do not make specific discipline at the point of time, often we will give no time.

Several safeguards are necessary in connection with any discipline. For instance, we must know there is no saving merit in the discipline itself. In a sort of paradox we encourage people to adopt a discipline, and at the same time, we tell them there is no merit in the discipline alone. We are never saved by a discipline. We are saved by the grace of God in Jesus Christ. The discipline simply makes us readily receptive so that the mercy and the grace of God can come into our lives in a significant degree.

Another safeguard is to make certain that persons are not encouraged to embrace the discipline before they are ready, because discipline will bring pressure on their lives. A person must be sure that he or she wants the pressure, or the pressure, when it comes, will cause resentment. We must be ready for discipline before embracing it. I have suggested to just as many people that they not adopt a discipline as I have that they adopt one. Safeguards are necessary.

The third thing I have learned over the period of nine years is that there is more danger in neglecting the discipline than there is in becoming self-righteous from keeping it. People who are critical say that if you adopt a discipline you run the risk of becoming smug and self-righteous, of developing spiritual pride. This is a danger, although when it happens, it is usually just a phase in a person's life—a very unattractive phase.

The danger at the opposite extreme is one of despair. A person who has faithfully kept the discipline begins to wonder whether or not God can ever really use him or her. "Have I made any progress at all over the last three years? Or am I just not the type? I had hoped that I would be, but I have made so little progress, is there any use of my keeping on?" So a person having kept the discipline may swing between these two opposite poles.

If we adopt the discipline and do not keep it—if we neglect it, which is the thing which most of us do—we become guilty of hypocrisy. We lay ourselves open to the charge and to the powerlessness of hypocrisy to a degree that a person who has never thought about a discipline does not encounter. The fear of becoming self-righteous may keep many of us from ever fully embracing a discipline. We never let ourselves loose. We never take off the brakes. We are going to have a tough time even if we do take off the brakes! If we have them on, it is hopeless.

If there is to be any power in a person's Christian life, there must be both a definite, full, acknowledged commitment and a specific, spelled-out discipline.

The fourth thing I have learned is that a period of prior preparation is essential for church membership. In our church we have five required classes: doctrine, Christian growth, ethics, and introductory courses in Old Testament and New Testament. The principal purpose is not merely to enable a person to gain useful knowledge but to ensure that, during the time spent within the framework of this fellowship, something intangible and undefinable may happen in the depths of her or his soul. The hope is that the seeker will meet and surrender to the living Christ.

The period of preparation allows time for people to sift their motivations and to ask, " Is Christ really calling me to this sort of ministry for him?" Those of us who have responded to this call know it to be the most wonderful thing in the world. We have been honored beyond any description. We are always wondering how it is that Christ could have called us. Well, is he really calling you? Or is there some other motivation? Do you feel guilty—that you ought to be a part of something which is constructive? Do you feel everybody ought to join some sort of church, and this is as good a one as you have stumbled across thus far? Or is God himself, the living Lord of all history and the God of the destiny of every one of us, laying his hand on you and saying, "I am calling you for the greatest thing which has ever touched your life. You must thank me through the eternities because I am calling you to this."

Is it Christ who is doing the calling? Are you sure that you want the closeness of people through the years or will this become irksome to you? As we move on into this deepening commitment, there will be no individual decisions, there will be no area of personal sovereignty. We belong to one another in a new relatedness. This is a family of faith. We are bound together irrevocably. Is this what you really want? This period gives us time to discover whether we truly want it. I am convinced that a period of preparation for church membership is absolutely essential.

The fifth thing I have learned is that growth depends upon this relatedness. It depends upon our being bound together in responsible relationships; God can best work in us as we hold all things in common. We hold our prayers in common. We hold our material resources in common. We make our decisions in common. As we hold our dreams in common with other Christian folk and build our common life together in this sort of relatedness, God's work is done.

One can do many things alone, but one thing a person cannot do alone is become a Christian. The history of Christian faith makes this clear. Now psychology and other social sciences are beginning to tell us that in this sort of relatedness new insights dawn, new power is granted, and people grow.

Relatedness implies a willingness to give concretely to the building up of common life. Not just being good, not just being fine Christians, but actually building up the common life. This means the concrete giving of time. How much time do you give to building up the common life? How much money do you give toward building up the common life? This means giving love toward building up the common life— praying to build up the common life. A person who hedges at the point of giving to the building up of the common life is cut off from great blessing and hurts the corporate witness of the church's life.

Relatedness means not only giving to the common life but also receiving from it. Sometimes receiving is more difficult for us than giving. How many times have you heard a person say, "This problem I shall work out alone. No one can help me at this point"? This is just an unlovely, ungracious way of saying, "I am breaking community; I can handle this myself." Often a real need arises in our individual lives—a financial need, a need to strengthen our family ties—and we are unwilling to let others (who would grow by sharing in that need) know what it is. Even as we must be willing to give to the common life, so must we be willing to receive from the common life. Through this relatedness come real power and growth.

A person cannot become a great Christian simply by attending services on Sunday morning, no matter how vital, wonderful, and filled with meaning those services may be.

The sixth thing I have discovered is that there is always danger in the Christian life. Growth entails danger. The time never comes when we can say, "I have it now; I've got the combination."

So often we feel that when we get hold of just the right book, it will provide the answer. Or we may be looking for just the right person with whom we can talk. Or we are waiting for the ecstatic experience that some day is going to come down to us out of the blue. Then we are really going to get started, and that is going to be it. But the right book in that sense will never come; the right person in that sense will never come; and the absolute experience will never occur. Wonderful books will come along, but they will simply open your life for the next book. A wonderful person who will mean life itself to you will come along, but he or she will prepare you for a deepening relationship with the next person.

The time never comes when we are finally sure of the combination, when we are out of danger in the Christian life, because new maturity brings a new dimension of freedom, and we can always misuse this freedom. It becomes enticing to take this new freedom and clutch it to ourselves, which is to misuse it. Scripture tells us that it was Lucifer, the most gifted of all the angels, who fell. That was Satan. Degradation comes with the misuse of freedom.

My conviction is that we in our church are in greater danger now than we were in the beginning. You have heard of the monastic cycle which goes like this: discipline produces abundance; abundance (unless we are very careful) destroys discipline. We are at the point of having a relative abundance of spiritual power, of spiritual dynamics, of pure joy because of what has been done for us. If we are not very careful, we will let the abundance destroy the discipline.

Another reason the situation is more dangerous now is that anyone seeking membership in the church today is not "put on the spot" as was a person in the early years, when only a very few people understood this church. In those days it was considered a weird organism. In this community we were breaking certain long-established denominational and racial patterns. We required a period of preparation for membership. There was a forthright demand for full commitment of life. And people wondered, What is this? Those who joined the church knew that the very next week they could expect to be backed into a corner to interpret it to people who did not understand and did not even want to understand. Every church needs members who are prepared to interpret its purpose and meaning.

Today there are many people who understand our church. We are no longer put on the spot in the same way. To become an "admirer of Jesus" (Kierkegaard's term) is much easier than to become a follower. In fact, it is possible now for a person to come into the cultural pattern of our church without having met the Head of the church. This is disastrous beyond description.

There is another danger. Our church is oriented now in the direction of losing its life in whatever places and causes God calls us to lose it. People will be going on mission. This is very good and very necessary—a movement which I believe to be inspired by God. The danger is that people will have a feeling of impermanence and will never get their roots down. They will be doing rather than being. They will never really belong. They will go before they will belong, without knowing they have missed the very kernel and heart of our life together. Christ is calling us to a lifetime belonging and a lifetime ministry with a quality of absoluteness that is not to be denied.

One thing more I have learned and know with all my soul is that it is difficult to maintain and enhance the exuberance and sense of wonder as time moves on and we become old in the faith. With aging in the faith we gain many things—experience, balance, depth—but so frequently we lose vitality. We no longer get to the boiling point which is necessary for Christian faith to be contagious. We simply engage in manipulating the church machinery. We grind it out week after week. Have you ever been depressed because of how much grinding of the machinery it takes to convert one puny Christian? The pot must boil so that there is an eagerness and an enthusiasm which come to be contagious.

Every single one of us is significant to somebody else. The people to whom we are significant will catch this thing from us if they know that we are, beyond the shadow of a doubt, absolutely devoted and loyal to the Lord Jesus Christ. But the trouble is that, in those moments which we think are "off moments," others decide whether or not we are truly committed. The times a person says, "I must talk to you," or when we are weeding the garden. Or working in an office. Grading a road. Nailing on a molding or painting a room. Cooking a meal. Speaking to a child. These are the times and places where the other person decides who we really are. There can be no "off moments" for Christians if our faith and its vitality are to be contagious.

I am committed more deeply now than ever before to these things which I have learned over the past nine years. I believe that the only hope of our world is the existence of Christian communities which are completely real, in which there is no artificiality, no equivocation.

We must come to the place where we can do what Jesus did, where we can watch the rich young ruler walk away and, with sorrow and an ache in our hearts, let him go until he can come back on the terms of Jesus Christ. We have been so afraid we might lose potential members that we have been willing to take them on their own terms. Then we wonder why the church is relatively impotent and doesn't have the power to transform human life, to shake society to its very roots.

I am committed more deeply than ever before to these things I have learned. As far as I know in my own mind and heart, I shall give myself to this sort of ministry throughout all of my life.

What is God calling you to do?

Part II

~⁓~

A New Kind of Leadership

2

The Nature of Christian Leadership

∾

In 1988, forty two years after the founding of The Church of the Saviour, Gordon continued to be deeply influenced by the time when, as a chaplain during World War II, he recognized the importance of leadership.

The first thirteen verses of the second chapter of the book of Acts describe the event of Pentecost. We, today, are trying to live out the spirit of Pentecost.

Beginning with the fourteenth verse, we have this statement:

> Peter stood up with the Eleven, raised his voice, and addressed them: "Fellow Jews, and all you who live in Jerusalem, mark this and give me a hearing. These men are not drunk, as you imagine; for it is only nine in the morning. No, this is what the prophet [Joel] spoke of: 'God says, "This will happen in the last days: I will pour out upon everyone a portion of my spirit; and your sons and daughters shall prophesy; your young men shall see visions, and your old men shall dream dreams. Yes, I will endue even my slaves, both men and women, with a portion of my spirit, and they shall prophesy. And I will show portents in the sky above, and signs on the earth below—blood and fire and drifting smoke. The sun shall be turned to darkness, and the moon to blood, before that great, resplendent day, the day of the Lord, shall come. And then, everyone who invokes the name of the Lord shall be saved."'" (Acts 2:14–21)

Then we skip a few verses and go to the thirty-seventh verse:

> When they heard this they were cut to the heart, and said to Peter and the apostles, "Friends, what are we to do?" "Repent,"

said Peter, "repent and be baptized, every one of you, in the
name of Jesus the Messiah for the forgiveness of your sins; and
you will receive the gift of the Holy Spirit. For the promise is to
you, and to your children, and to all who are far away, everyone whom the Lord our God may call." (Acts 2:37–39)

Whenever God calls a person, that call always involves leadership—
the sort of leadership which is crucial for our nation and for our own
community.

A number of us are thinking especially about leadership these days
because for several years we have nurtured a dream of a school for
servant leaders. Very soon a fence will go up around the parking lot at
the corner of Columbia Road and construction will begin on the
building in which the Servant Leadership School will be housed. There
will be approximately eight months of construction. In April or May of
1989 we hope to open to the public the school that we have been
planning for many, many years.

The future of the church depends upon gifted leadership. This community depends entirely upon the sort of people who are now in our
School of Christian Living preparing for leadership in this community.
And our country is dependent upon the leadership which we are praying
for and working toward. As we think about our country, we long for a
new kind of leadership to guide us into God's future for our nation.

The biblical assumption is that every Christian is called by God and
that, by virtue of this call by Yahweh, every person is called to leadership. Therefore, "call" equals "leadership." Greenleaf says that a leader
is "one who goes out ahead." And if he or she is an effective leader,
there will be someone to follow. If we go out ahead and no one
follows, we are not giving effective leadership. We need to be persons
who will inspire others to follow.

Moses was called to liberate God's people from their slavery in Egypt to
a new, responsible nationhood. For Moses, to be called meant that he was
called to leadership. And my call, if I am faithful to it, by its very nature
involves leadership. Your call, if you are faithful to it, involves leadership.

To begin to see ourselves as leaders is very difficult for us. Not to see
ourselves in this light saves us from accepting responsibility. Many
people have said to me: "I've never conceived myself as a leader. I
want to be a good follower." An amazing way to slip out from under
responsibility.

Christian leadership requires many component qualities. Within my
own life I am seeking to develop four of these dimensions. If you aspire

to leadership in the kingdom of God, you will want to develop them in your life.

The first is vision. The ancient prophet recorded God as saying, "Where there is no vision, the people perish" (Prov. 29:18, *KJV*). And we reread the prophecy previously quoted in Acts:

> "This will happen in the last days. I will pour out upon everyone a portion of my spirit [not upon just a few gifted ones]; and your sons and daughters shall prophesy; your young men shall see visions and your old men shall dream dreams." (Acts 2:17–18)

Thus, one crucial mark of the Pentecostal experience is the seeing of visions and the dreaming of dreams—all of which sounds so otherworldly, so superfluous in today's world. However, this most crucial gift of the leader is the capacity to see new possibilities, new combinations of energy and life coming together and to see now, in imagination, that which is not yet but which ought to be.

In light of that which is, the vision seems to be fantastic. We are daily confronted with what is: the threat of nuclear destruction; the unemployment of youth, especially black youth in this city; the plight of the elderly, their loneliness and their helplessness. We see homeless people, with the number of homeless families growing daily; the injustice of our criminal justice system; the problem of drugs in our nation; and the list goes on interminably. We face the inability of people to care for the weak and the helpless, and the church in many of its expressions seems fat and bloated and mired down in almost complete paralysis.

Are these the dominant conditions that you see? Do you feel that you must adjust to these conditions? Is this the real situation? Believing that you perceive it so clearly, do you see yourself as a realist determined that no one is going "to put anything over" on you? Almost everybody sees things this way. There is nothing new about it. If this is true for you, few stimulating juices of excitement will flow because of your self-defined "realism."

Suppose, instead, that you see not the threat of nuclear destruction but a world reorganized, restructured, and totally free of the war system. Suppose you see not the woeful unemployment of youth but a society restructured with enough of us working voluntarily so that every unemployed youth would have employment. We would realize that it is unthinkable for the potential gift of any human being to go unused.

Go down the list. What do you see? What is the real future? Does the present contain within it the possibility of something utterly different?

When God declared that he/she would do a new thing, was God lying? Did the resurrection occur? Is Christ coming again? Is the present just the womb of the new?

I believe that the vision that I see—so different from what is—is real. "Visionary" equals "realist." And I must adjust to the things that I envision in my most imaginative moments. For they will surely be.

Vision, then, is the capacity to see that which ought to be but is not yet. And to see it clearly. Moses saw what was fantastic, that which was not yet. Saul was able to see that which was not yet and which should have been. Everybody who is called is given the capacity to see the "not yet" but the "that which ought to be." And because it ought to be, it will be.

Another facet of this seeing is just as important as the seeing itself. It is a very crucial step. It is that moment—and the process leading up to that moment—when you inwardly say: "I will take on the vision that has been given me. I will assume ultimate responsibility for it. There are, of course, people better qualified to do it. But that is not the point. The vision has been given to me by God. I can see a little segment of the world which can be utterly different. I will take on the vision. I will act on it. Then, if that better qualified person who is called comes along and will take it over, I will be freed to do something else. In the meantime, I will do it. I will be the instrument of God for making it happen. I will let this thing rest on me." Such a response is quite different from just seeing the vision.

> Then I heard the Lord saying, Whom shall I send? Who will go
> for me? And I answered, Here am I; send me. He said, Go, and
> tell this people: . . . (Isa. 6:8–9)

Very simple. I'll go. I will do it. This vision that I am seeing, I will let it rest on me. And I will see that it becomes implemented.

Ultimate responsibility means that I am not "helping" some other strong person so that his or her task will be easier. Mine is not just supportive help, though this will be given again and again. Others will help me and I will help them. This is very important. But in the area of the vision for which I am assuming ultimate responsibility, others are helping me, rather than my helping them.

In a time when dependence is one of our major sicknesses, assumption of responsibility is extremely difficult and rare. If I long to be dependent and to depend on strong, significant others, it will be hard to give up the possibility of having another carry me.

A mark of assumption of ultimate responsibility is the diminishing, if not the elimination of grumbling, complaining, and blaming.

> The Israelites complained to Moses and Aaron in the wilderness and said, "If only we had died at the LORD's hand in Egypt, where we sat around the fleshpots and had plenty of bread to eat! [Give us slavery if we can eat!] But you have brought us out into this wilderness, to let this whole assembly starve to death." (Exod. 16:3)

Moses had assumed the responsibility of leadership, but the people he was leading were grumbling, complaining, and shifting to Moses and Aaron responsibility for their plight. Anyone who assumes responsibility, takes it on, does very little grumbling. You may not quit grumbling, but at least you diminish it and you know that it is not creative.

To grumble in the right context is very important. Get someone who can hear it, so you can work it through, because you are hurting. But at the point of leadership, you assume ultimate responsibility.

One who has assumed ultimate responsibility for a vision does not become defensive—does not explain the seeming slowness of progress by suggesting that this is just the wrong time in history for the thing to come off. Nor is the excuse made that the necessary support was not given because a more favorable combination of significant others did not show up.

So many people say: "It's just that the people didn't respond. I sounded the call. But the people didn't show up. And as for the ones who did show up, you could never have done anything with that crowd." Or, "There wasn't enough money."

My task—your task—is to generate the interest, whatever it takes. My task is to find the money, no matter how astronomical the amount seems. My task is to get close enough to Jesus Christ for him to do through me what he wants to do, which is the call that he has placed on my life. My task is to develop those leadership skills and sensitivities which are now lacking in my leadership. And they can be developed if I will make the necessary earnest effort. So the first dimension of leadership is the capacity to see a vision, and then to accept it.

What a big jump there is between that seeing and the acceptance! We make that jump, saying: "I don't know how to do it. The task seems impossible. I don't know how to do it, but I will do it. If I can't do it, I will be faithful unto death. I will hold that vision. People will know that I'm holding it. And one day it will happen."

The second dimension of any great leadership is hope. And hope is clearly related to vision. John Gardner has this to say:

> When the regeneration of societies has been achieved, as it often has been over the course of history, the agents of that achievement have been people with the capacity to hope. (The opposite of hope is cynicism and disillusionment.) . . . Among the people who express the greatest cynicism and disillusionment today is what one might call the "crypto-utopian." Hidden beneath the layers of bitterness and defeatism is a yearning soul that believes that people and society are perfectible, and is outraged that we have fallen so short.
>
> In truth, the crypto utopians have a marvelously self-indulgent game going. If you expect perfectionism, and will settle for nothing less, you can scorn the efforts of imperfect women and men to achieve what turns out to be less than perfection. You can feel wise and superior without ever getting out of your chair.
>
> Utopianism, whether hidden or open, places an awesome burden on those who must strive to keep our imperfect society from becoming even more imperfect.[1]

Despair feels that it's no use. Our best efforts will come to nothing. That attitude will never generate the force to solve our problems. And the prophecy will fulfill itself.

In *War and Peace* Prince André says of Austerlitz, "Our loss was not much greater than that of the French, but we said to ourselves very early in the engagement that we would lose it, and we did lose it."[2] In other words, we lost because we told ourselves we would lose. Militarily it was not quite that simple. But the point is clear. Fatalism saps the will and produces the situation it prophesies.

Hope is a form of faith and tends to produce what it sees. Despair is a form of faith and tends to produce what it sees.

As a leader in the family, the neighborhood, the work scene, the church, you are nurturing some combination of life that really depends on you. It is crucial how you see this combination of life—whether you see it with hope or whether you see it without hope, just trying to survive day by day. There will never be a dearth of people, close friends, who will inform you that the whole thing is going to pieces: our faith community is in terrible shape; the institutions that we are nurturing are at a low ebb.

What do you see? Do you see dominantly the problems of the moment? Or do you see dominantly the new possibilities growing out of the present ordeal? If you give way to cynicism and despair, many will seize the problem as an excuse for quitting. There are people who are quitting the fray every day because of despair and cynicism. They simply cannot take it any longer. Others are hanging in there and staying on in the fray for another day because they have hope.

If you as a leader view the problem with hope, many will be challenged to get on with it. Hope, the indispensable ingredient of leadership, is the key.

Can you imagine what it was like for Moses between the ninth and the tenth plagues? He stood his ground. Then came the tenth plague followed by the release of the slaves. Suppose he had quit at the end of the ninth plague!

Or suppose that you had been with him there at the Red Sea, before the waters parted. You could readily have understood if Moses—with the water in front of him and all of Pharaoh's military might behind him—had said to the people, "Well, listen. We got this far. We tried. But this is a terrible situation. So get ready to die, or at least go back to serve Pharaoh."

In that impossible situation Moses said: "God is faithful. He will never leave or forsake us. So remain poised and alert, and you will see a demonstration of God's power."

Situations like that happen every day. Whether there is a victory— whether there is a crossing—depends upon whether or not you or I will be able to hang in there with hope in that moment, hope against the critical odds.

Yours may at some time be the only voice of hope, the only one declaring that all is well. Around your lone voice fearful, disillusioned, discouraged people will gather. Hope is absolutely essential as an ingredient of great leadership if we are going to take people where no one has gone—into the "not yet," into the new.

The third ingredient is what I would call empathic universalism, as opposed to empathic provincialism. The great leader sees and feels himself or herself as a part of the whole—identified with the totality.

David Rothman says that a basic change occurred in our society about 1966 when the formulation of Black Power took place. Black Power rhetoric, unlike that of Martin Luther King, Jr., looked first not to brotherhood but to separatism. It was premised not upon a mutuality of interest shared by all members of society, but upon basic conflicts in the society.

In no uncertain terms (and I can surely understand it) blacks were admonished to become organized, get control of their economic

institutions, their own political institutions, their own community, if they
ever expected to achieve substantial gains in the white racist society.

In many ways the changeover from dreams of brotherhood to
establishment of Black Power is paradigmatic of the changes that have
transformed our society from 1966 until the present. Black Power
became the strategy that every minority group in our society attempted
to emulate. In the organization of welfare rights, the movement for
prisoners' rights, mental patients' rights, the rights of the retarded, the
rights of children—this same attitude prevails.

The commonalities are clear: Organize your own special interest group,
press your own demands. The perspective is not the perspective of the
common welfare but the needs of the particular group. The intellectual
premises are not based on unity but on conflict. It is "us" *vs.* "them."

Empathic universalism has no exclusiveness in caring but rather
intense caring at the point of the totality. I will, of course, have intense
caring at the point of my own particular call, but that does not reduce
or limit my caring in other areas. Deep, intense caring at one point
enhances my caring for the whole commonwealth.

Provincialism limits my caring. The feeling often is that if I make my
circle small enough, life will seem safer and neater. So I put boundaries
around my caring: "My mission group is really my church; I don't care
about the faith community." Or "My faith community is what really
matters. The whole Church of the Saviour doesn't matter." Or "The
Church of the Saviour is all that matters. The larger body of Christ is
not my concern." Or "The body of Christ is all that matters. The
unredeemed world is not my concern." Empathic universalism means
that we belong to the totality, in empathy, in our emotions, in our
feeling tones.

The great leader never feels it is us *versus* them. He or she is for
everybody. To be for one interest group is never to be against another. To
be for those without power is surely not to be against those with power.

Provincialism occurs frequently in personal situations of conflict. We
hear the tale of two of our friends. One seems to be the victim. One
seems to be right, the other wrong, and we easily withdraw empathy
from the "villain."

Suppose our assessment of the situation is accurate, although this
may be highly questionable. The villain of this moment is the victim of
an earlier moment. Because I'm deeply for one, why should I be
against the other? Why can't I be deeply for both? If I am absolutely

unyielding in my attitude favoring one over the other, I am diminishing the freedom of attitude on the part of other people. In so doing I am limiting my capacity for leadership.

I can find ultimate meaning in my call and in that of which I am a part—and at the same time enhance other facets of the whole to which I belong. I will never hurt the particular that I'm called to by being a part of the whole and enhancing the whole. What I need for my particular will always flow back to me if I am giving myself to the whole. We must do nothing that in any way diminishes another.

The fourth dimension of leadership concerns waiting. Although very hard to describe, I think this dimension is even more important than vision, which earlier was said to be the most important.

Jesus is our example in everything, including leadership. W. H. Vanstone, a member of the Doctrine Commission of the Church of England, in his book *The Stature of Waiting,* talks about two phases of Jesus' adult ministry through which Jesus glorifies the Father and the Father glorifies the Son.

In the first phase Jesus is doing the "mighty works" of the kingdom. He is healing, feeding, caring, loving, and building the community of his disciples. He is in control. The townspeople try to throw him over the cliff, but he walks unscathed through their midst. He is exceedingly active, and they are not able to stop him because his time has not yet come.

Almost at the end, according to Vanstone, he works out a brilliant strategy. He is hoping to win the response of the leadership of his nation. If the kingdom that he is trying to bring is going to come, it must be accepted not only by the weak and the poor but also by the people who are in control—the power structure.

The strategy, according to Vanstone's interpretation, is that Jesus will go publicly into Jerusalem, and by being public will cause one of two things to happen. Either the authorities will be so threatened that they will have to do away with him, or, because he would be demonstrating that the people were supporting this newness, this new kingdom, those in political power might accept his program. Thus Jesus brings matters to a head, hoping they will accept. After that Sunday, and especially after that Thursday night, he is "handed over." The task now is not one of brilliant strategy but one of doing nothing except waiting.

That waiting is another dimension of glorifying the Father. The way it is presented in the New Testament, the Passion is not primarily suffering. It is not pain; it is not suffering; it is not death primarily—

although all those things are a part of it. The Passion involves the choosing, the willingness to be handed over, to be dependent upon the response of other people.

So the question comes: Are we willing to be handed over? Jesus was willing to be handed over; he was willing to leave it in the hands of others as to whether he would be accepted or whether he would be rejected. He became totally vulnerable. The God of the universe became totally vulnerable on our behalf, willing for everything that he held dear to hang in the balance.

Are we willing, after we have done all that we know to hold the vision, and to carry it with hope, and to let it be a part of the totality, and to give it our best—are we willing then simply to wait when we have done all? And simply to suffer, and to let our vicarious suffering be the means by which God ultimately brings the kingdom?

Love always creates a situation where we must wait upon the other. Always. You cannot produce the results, if you are loving. You create a situation which depends upon the response of the other. The other person may or may not respond. And the age in which you are giving leadership may or may not respond. Nevertheless, you give your life. You dedicate it as totally as you know how to dedicate it. And you wait, in trust, for God.

The amazing thing about Jesus was that he was willing to be handed over, to wait and accept the consequences, even unto the point of death. In his case the consequence was rejection. But he willingly handed himself over.

Jesus' kind of leadership is the kind of leadership needed in our time if our society is going to survive; if the kingdom is going to come in; if the church is going to be the church that Jesus is calling the church to be. If our society is to be that new society that God longs for it to be, this kind of leadership is required.

Much is at stake. God is calling you, and God is calling me, to something quite beyond what we have ever been or ever done before.

Notes

[1] John W. Gardner, *Morale* (New York: W.W. Norton and Co., 1978), pp. 150-51.

[2] Leo Tolstoy, *War and Peace,* part ten, 1812, chapter 17.

3

Servant Leadership

~

In 1989 the Festival Center (the building housing the Servant Leadership School) was completed. On this occasion, Gordon again reflected on the nature of Christian leadership.

The opening ceremonies for the Festival Center and the Servant Leadership School have been occasions the significance of which is, I believe, beyond our comprehension. What is going to take place as a result of what has already happened will make a difference in the life of the world church for decades to come.

Dr. James Forbes was with us for our celebration. He excites my heart more than any preacher in America. What amazes me is that oftentimes a person from another part of the world can better understand what is happening than those of us who are here planning it and working with it. As Dr. Forbes spoke to us, somehow he was able to touch the nuances of who we want to be, and he said it for us at a level which was deep and profound. He emphasized some of the qualities of servanthood that are important and meaningful to us.

We are grateful, too, for other persons who have been very important to our life—persons who have been a part of the Ministry of Money and have helped to build the foundations of so many of the visions that God has given us.

We have with us George Lagerquist who, in memory of his wife, gave the gift of the chapel and its furnishings (or, the furnishings to be—it is not yet furnished). Already, under Allen Holt's leadership, worship takes place there three times a day at eight, twelve, and five o'clock; people working in the building, neighborhood people, students who come from many different places, and all of us who find it possible to be there are engaged in a ministry of prayer. At times other than the set times of worship, the chapel is a sacramental place where people can go to be alone, be still and pray.

In addition to the gift of the chapel a little lending library has been given to the Festival Center by an anonymous donor in honor of our beloved Thelma Hemker. The dedication of the library to Thelma will, in our eyes, lend to it an especial aura and value through the years to come.

These two are very special gifts, and there are others too numerous to name.

Since we have celebrated the opening ceremonies of the Servant Leadership School and received with appreciation gifts which in themselves are examples of the generosity of true servants, I find it appropriate to consider Jesus' concepts of servanthood as given in the tenth chapter of Mark:

> They were on the road, going up to Jerusalem, Jesus leading the way; and the disciples were filled with awe, while those who followed behind were afraid. [It is amazing what fear does to us.] He took the Twelve aside and began to tell them what was to happen to him. "We are now going to Jerusalem," he said; "and the Son of Man will be given up to the chief priests and the doctors of the law; they will condemn him to death and hand him over to the foreign power. He will be mocked and spat upon, flogged and killed; and three days afterwards, he will rise again. (Mark 10:32-34)

They were probably more fearful after he finished that little speech than they had been before. So often we tell people, "You shouldn't be afraid." But Jesus was telling them what was really going to happen.

> James and John, the sons of Zebedee, approached him and said, "Master, we should like you to do us a favour." "What is it you want me to do?" he asked. They answered, "Grant us the right to sit in state with you, one at your right and the other at your left." Jesus said to them, "You do not understand what you are asking. Can you drink the cup that I drink, or be baptized with the baptism I am baptized with?" [And in their ignorance and inexperience they answered,] "We can."
> Jesus said, "The cup that I drink you shall drink, and the baptism I am baptized with shall be your baptism; but to sit at my right or left is not for me to grant; it is for those to whom it has already been assigned."

When the other ten heard this, they were indignant with
James and John. [I find it encouraging that there were problems
within that little mission group. And this problem involved
John—the beloved disciple who was supposed to have such
deep insight.] Jesus called them to him and said, "You know
that in the world the recognized rulers lord it over their subjects,
and their great men make them feel the weight of authority.
That is not the way with you; among you [within this new
community, within this new approach to life] whoever wants to
be great must be your servant, and whoever wants to be first
must be the willing slave of all. For even the Son of Man did not
come to be served but to serve, and to give up his life as a
ransom for many." (Mark 10:35-45)

My feeling is that each of us lives by some vision—perhaps a de-
pressing vision, or a very limited vision, or a vision that everything is
going to pieces. But each of us lives by a vision, conscious or unconscious. Should it be a dark vision moving toward disintegration and
chaos, we will be fearful. If it is a larger vision, a universal vision, a
vision of the kingdom, and we really believe that it is going to take
place, we will be filled with hope. Hope is the feeling, the confidence,
that the vision which is the biblical vision will really occur.

The biblical vision, the vision of the Shalom, is the vision of the
totality. God is the God of a people called to be a blessing to all the
nations, all tribes, all combinations of people. No one is going to be
excluded. All are moving toward this Shalom. Everybody shares and
participates, is a part of it—no one is left out. This vision is one of
universal justice and peace.

The closer we get to the biblical God—the closer we get to Jesus—
the more we participate in the whole, draw our nourishment from
giving to the whole, and enhance the common good. There are no
partial loyalties. We never give ourselves to one flag. Patriots are
persons who give themselves to a flag, one flag. But persons who are
close to God—evolved human beings who have grown close to Jesus—
never fly a partial flag. Under a universal flag we move toward universalism until every partial loyalty is abandoned.

When we are moving in this direction, it becomes increasingly
difficult to draw from the common good or from the pool of resources.
We may know that we are strong enough to take goodies out of the
common jar—that they are there for the taking—and that at one level
we can get by with it. We may be strong and smart enough to take

from the common till without anyone's catching up with us. But the whole mood and tenor of our lives have come to be that of wanting to give into the common pool, not taking or holding on to anything more than we really need. And the common good comes to be so real and important that taking from it and holding on to more than our share are unthinkable. We simply want to contribute to the whole. We do not want to hold unequal power over anybody. It is not satisfying. So we come to perceive ourselves as part of the whole. To weaken the whole is ultimately to destroy ourselves.

We sense and feel keenly about the whole because we know that everything is interconnected. Any gift we have is seen as a gift to enhance the total family of humanity. We are here to move the totality toward the Shalom, the completion, the fulfillment, the coming into her or his own of every person who is living and has ever lived, and every person who will ever be born into the future.

In reality, we are not separate individuals, as we often feel ourselves to be. We are meshed, we are intertwined, we flow into and out of one another and all others. There is no way to fix the boundaries. The Christ who flows into us is simultaneously flowing into the billions of the world's people. Where do we end and they begin? Millions of cells in the human body make up the body's totality. All are working harmoniously on behalf of the whole, unless some of the cells become sick or cancerous. Each of us is part of God's total people, and we cannot separate ourselves from the totality.

Until awareness of this universal belonging dawns upon us we are a hindrance to the human family. It is a great day when the boundaries drop. We are part of others, and they are a part of us. We are constantly flowing into them. We cannot protect ourselves from their sickness and pain and brokenness. Nor can others protect themselves from ours. All become united. The common life of humanity is not an ideal, not something that would be just wonderful if we could but realize it. The universal quality of life happens to be a reality, and we utterly defeat ourselves when we violate that premise. We can live in the illusion of separateness, but it is an illusion.

The overall vision of God and the kingdom gives assurance that all of humanity is going to be freed from its present bondage and is going to be reconciled with the source of its life—God—and with one another. And each individual or cell in the body will know total, inner reconciliation and total fulfillment of all of its potential.

The symbol of fulfillment of this vision is the banquet, or the feast, and is used frequently to represent the culmination in unity. We are all going to be together, and there is going to be good food, and good fellowship, and all the people of the world are going to be there—in that ultimate reconciliation, the wedding feast of the Lamb.

A basic question, of course, is how often or how deeply do we see this vision as really happening so that we live by it? We say the prayer, "Thy kingdom come," but when we pray do we see it as happening? Or as we say, "Thy kingdom come," do we feel that everything is going to pieces? Do we ever feel our prayer moving all of humanity toward the Shalom?

The vision is so fantastic that believing it requires supernatural faith. The nature of our sin is so profound and our alienation is so deep that the vision is seldom taken seriously. I can believe the vision when I am in the midst of my community. But all one has to do to shake that belief is to walk down the streets of Adams-Morgan, down Columbia Road, as I did this morning. I saw at least ten people—addicted, homeless, hopeless—just as those who work in the neighborhood see them or others like them every hour of the day.

In the midst of all the negative situations and data, there is no easy way to hold that universal vision—the vision that God, using us, is going to usher in the Shalom—that the kingdom is really coming—that one day justice and peace will cover the earth as the waters cover the sea.

Hope is the deep conviction that the vision will come to fruition; the confidence that it will really happen. Let us suppose that we have this conviction, and we want to use the few remaining years of our lives to move the vision forward. What is the power, what kind of leadership will move it toward its destiny? Our term is *servant leadership*. By this we mean the special power and energy of a person and a community which draw the whole body of humanity to its appointed end, releasing God's nature and thus God's power. Our natural understanding cannot comprehend God's nature. "For my thoughts are not your thoughts, and your ways are not my ways" (Isa. 55:8). There is a fundamental difference.

Jesus, in the Scripture, says,

> "You know that in the world the recognized rulers lord it over their subjects, and their great men make them feel the weight of their authority [prestige, status, dominating power, the capacity to stay on top]. That is not the way with you; among you,

whoever wants to be great must be your servant, and whoever
wants to be first must be the willing slave of all. For even the
Son of Man did not come to be served but to serve, and to give
up his life as a ransom for many." (Mark 10:42-45)

In speaking with Don Martin this morning I had an interesting
insight. Don was referring to what Dr. Forbes said yesterday: "I always
had a little trouble with this passage of Scripture because I didn't want
to be least in order that one day I might be first. That just didn't sound
right to me—having this thing reversed one day as the method of
getting to be first. But now I understand it more deeply. You can't get
to where you want to be by exercising dominating power. But if we can
learn the meaning of service and being least, we will understand what it
truly means to be a human being. Released and freed from the desire
for all those things we formerly wanted, we then become 'first' as far as
the quality of our lives is concerned. Moreover, the idea of dominating
anyone in the future would be out of the question."

In accordance with God's nature this is the way the universe works.
This is what was incarnated in the very being of Jesus. "He came not
to be served, but to serve, and to give up his life as a ransom for
many."

We begin to see this as a "descending way" as opposed to an
"ascending way." Henri Nouwen, in his *Letters to Marc About Jesus*,
has a chapter entitled "Jesus, the Descending God." Writing from the
L'Arche Community in Canada, Henri says:

> I may say that the contrast between my university life and my
> life here at L'Arche is greater than I realized at first. The
> contrast isn't so much between intelligent students and mentally
> handicapped people, as in the ascending style of the university
> and the descending style of L'Arche.
>   You might say that at Yale and Harvard they are principally
> interested in upward mobility. Whereas here, they believe in the
> importance of downward mobility. That's the radical difference.
> And I notice in myself how difficult it is to change directions on
> the ladder.[1]

In the Gospel it is quite obvious that Jesus chose the descending
way. He chose it not once but over and over again. At each critical
moment he deliberately sought the way downward. Even though at
twelve years of age he was alert and precocious, already listening to the
teachers at the Temple and questioning them, he was submissive to his

parents and stayed up to his thirtieth year in the little-respected town of Nazareth. We call these the hidden years of Jesus.

Even though he was without sin, Jesus began his public life by joining the ranks of sinners who were being baptized by John in the Jordan. If you were especially gifted, don't you think you would have said to John, "I'm going to bypass this little arrangement. It's all right for these other characters but, you know, I've got hold of this"? But Jesus said, "I want to join the others in this rite of baptism." And even though he was full of divine power, he believed that changing stones into bread, seeking popularity, and being counted among the great ones of the earth were temptations. Again and again he opted for what is small and hidden and poor, and declined to wield influence.

His many miracles always serve to express his profound compassion for suffering humanity. Never are they attempts to call attention to himself. As a rule, he even forbids those he has cured to talk to others about it. And, as Jesus' life continues to unfold, he becomes increasingly aware that he has been called to fulfill his vocation in suffering and death.

In all this it becomes plain to us that God has willed to show his love for the world by descending more and more deeply into human frailty. The more conscious Jesus becomes of the mission entrusted to him by the Father, the more he realizes that mission will make him poorer and poorer. He, who was rich, for our sakes became poor. And finally he hangs on a cross, crying out with a loud voice, "My God, my God, why hast thou forsaken me?" (Mark 15:34). Only then do we know how far God has gone to show us his love. For it is then that Jesus not only reached his utmost poverty but also showed us God's utmost love.

God is the descending God. The movement is down, down, down, until it finds the sickest, the most afflicted, the most helpless, the most alienated, the most cut off.

The truest symbols that we have of Jesus are the lamb—the lamb led to the slaughter; a sheep before its shearers being dumb. Total poverty: a dumb sheep, the Lamb of God, and the Servant Christ kneeling with a towel and a basin, washing feet on the eve of his crucifixion. The weeping Christ riding into Jerusalem on a donkey. These are the symbols, the images of the surrender of power and control, wanting no person to feel the weight of authority. (And how we throw our authority around!) No subtle or overt lording it over anyone but a longing for leastness. Not only to be with the least of the least, the poorest of the poor, but to become the least of the least.

Being with the least is difficult enough, but even more difficult is that other step of becoming the least of the least. "As you did it to one of the least of these my brethren, you did it to me" (Matt. 25:40, *RSV*). And as you do it to the least, you begin to become the least. You become a part of their lives. Our trouble is that we live in a debilitating dichotomy. We listen to this "weakness" stuff, this "servant" stuff, and we name the symbols. But we just do not believe that the way to God, the way of fulfillment, is the downward way, the way of descent.

We spend our best thinking and energies on the upward way and are distressed if we slip a bit and are not recognized or appreciated. And if sometimes through God's help we manage a miracle, we hope the recipient will tell everybody. We do not tell the person not to tell. (Or we tell them not to tell, but we hope they do not listen to us!) We want our reputation to be enhanced, we want to be known as the one who can perform miracles in Christ's name. It is hard for us to imagine why Jesus told his healed friends not to tell anybody.

Although we don't really believe in this "weakness" stuff, we have a problem. What was it that captured our hearts? It was that figure dying on a cross. That is what got to us. We sing, "The very dying form of one who suffered there for me."

The closer we get to the end of life, the more meaningful the symbols of weakness become. I have noticed this time and time again: people of power appreciate more and more the images of weakness as they draw closer to the end.

If the Lamb of God, the dumb sheep, the form of the Servant Christ giving his life away for others—for me—if those deep expressions of reality captured my spirit, literally broke my hard heart of stone and gave me a heart of flesh, ended my captivity and delivered my spirit, why do I think that the expression of authority or power or success or efficiency is going to break anybody's heart? That which released love within my own being is just what is going to release love in other hearts. It is the only thing that will do it. We do not say that Jesus lived a great life but ended that life poorly. The crowning event of his life was the death that he died, the poverty, the leastness of those final hours. The death is the glory.

In John 17:24 Jesus is praying, and he says, "Father, I desire that these men, who are thy gift to me . . . "—*gift*, although he knows that they will betray and desert him. When people disagree with me, betray or desert me, I certainly do not consider them as gift. I resent them. But Jesus is saying, while they are deserting him, "Father, I thank you for the gift of these men to me, and I pray that they may be with me at the cross, watching me die, because that will be the glory. And I don't want them to miss it. Not only would I like their support, but I would like them to witness the crowning glory of my life" (paraphrased).

This expression of total poverty—the dying on the cross—was the total descent and thus the height of the glory. We sing, "In the cross of Christ I glory, towering o'er the wrecks of time."[2]

This life, when it reaches the depths, as it reached those depths in Jesus, explodes into infinite newness. The only man ever resurrected was the one who hit the bottom and knew total poverty. He was the one who was resurrected, no one else. And so we have a new injection into the life stream of humanity—a totally new enhancement of the common good.

The ascending way never explodes into newness. It inevitably reaches its pinnacle of fame, authority, and power by absorbing that which should never have been arrogated to it. We hold on to certain names, remember and sometimes envy their accomplishments, and write much of our history around those names. We don't write history about the poor, the real people. We write it about those names. But, in the words of Neville Watson, they don't make us want to "walk tall in the faith." They don't release love into the common family.

Suppose the only God that exists is the descending God. Suppose the only way we can know God is to go down, to go to the bottom. Suppose the only way to be reconciled to God is to be reconciled with the least, who are at the bottom. If God is going down and we are going up, it is obvious that we are going in different directions. And we will not know him. We will be evading God and missing the whole purpose of our existence.

Jesus said, "And I, when I am lifted up . . . "—lifted up on the cross, which was the bottom of the descent. If I reach bottom and give up my being totally into God's will and purpose for love of the world's people, then I—"will draw all men to myself" (John 12:32, *RSV*).

To reach bottom is to exert an infinite pull on the heartstrings of humanity. Why do you think Mother Teresa has been able to reach out and embrace us all? Why do you think Jean Vanier has been able to reach out and embrace us all? Because they know something about being at the bottom.

If I can take this way, and if you can take this way—and if we are lifted up—we will draw all people to him who was lifted up. As we hit bottom there will be an explosion releasing infinite energy for the common good. And we will hasten the moment when justice and peace will cover the earth as the waters cover the sea.

Are we ready? Will we be those servant people, bringing in the Shalom of God by making the downward journey?

Notes

[1] Henri Nouwen, *Letters to Marc About Jesus* (New York: Harper & Row, 1988), p. 41.

[2] "In the Cross of Christ I Glory," words by John Bowring, The United Methodist Hymnal (Nashville, Tenn.: The United Methodist Publishing Company, 1992), p. 295.

4

The Ministry and the Ministries

~

*In 1958 Gordon was invited by the Ecumenical Institute of the World
Council of Churches at Chateau de Bossey, near Geneva, Switzer-
land, to interpret the ministry of The Church of the Saviour and its
focus. This address was given in response to that invitation.*

What is the ministry of the church? What are the ministries of the
church? How does the ministry differ from the ministries? After having
been given some insight into these questions, how does one proceed to
embody, in the concrete historical situation, the light God has given?

My comments on these questions are those of one who has sought
to take the thinking and experience of theologians and sociologists and
let the Word of God transpose them for my own particular time and
place and calling. My illustrations are from the lives of the people I
know best. I am aware of the danger of overemphasizing particularities.
On the other hand, even at the expense of being misunderstood, I am
eager to throw into sharp focus any light which may enable others to
see more clearly.

We may consider these questions on a number of different levels.
Some will elicit endless discussion and no confrontation. But some
issues that arise in living situations—questions difficult to resolve merely
by logical thought—can be resolved by the enabling grace of God.

My deep conviction is that evangelism begins with a local congregation which, in some degree, visibly embodies the characteristic
marks of the church, the comprehensive mark of which is that of
servant. The church is a community of those who have entered into the
life, death, and resurrection of Jesus Christ. This radical experience in
Christ makes one a new creation and binds one in love to a new
community. The community, then, is in actuality one, holy, catholic,

and apostolic, living in the unmerited grace of God. Truly freed in some degree from its natural compulsive striving for justification, it is at least relatively free to love and to serve. But these are generalities. Let us be concrete.

Love for one another in Christ—obedience to the command of Christ, "Love one another as I have loved you"—develops a *style* of community life having many facets, as does the life of a family. A common life is shared, a real "life together" where members have unlimited liability for one another. This ideal life in Christ can scarcely be described. It must be experienced. Life in our particular community is symbolized by such things as:

- loan funds for emergency needs—the purchase or building of a new home, the establishing of new businesses or the propping up of old ones;
- outright gifts in times of crisis or peculiar need, such as sickness, financial mismanagement, or funds required for a university education;
- development of a fellowship and retreat center for work, play, and retreat;
- opportunity for each person to be related intimately to others in the study of the Bible and in prayer;
- twice-a-year festivals celebrating our common life under Christ;
- frequent contact in one another's homes.

All this life is nourished by the preaching of the Word and the sharing in holy communion.

Community life is known as *koinonia*. This life can continue and deepen only as it expresses itself in *diakonia*—in witness to the world and in the world. Always there is the danger that community life will turn in on itself, that a sort of spiritual cannibalism will occur. If this happens—and it is a perennial temptation—all is lost. God, by grace, makes us part of a community which, knowing an eternal dimension, in some sense transcends our fragmented society in order that we may remain in that fragmented society. Yet we remain in a different way— now not pulled, torn, crushed, and depersonalized by it—not as victims of it but as renewers of it. We are now agents of One who is already there.

Perhaps two things should always be occurring. First, lay ministers, as representatives of the colony of heaven by their style of life and by their verbal witness, are always channeling God's grace to those with whom they live and work and in the spontaneous groupings in which they find themselves. In one way or another they are always declaring, "We have seen Jesus." Others are brought to share this new dimension of life granted to the Christian. To withhold this from any person open to it would be to deny our apostolate. However, those who come to share this new life in Christ are immediately driven more deeply into the world's life.

Second, there should be a ministry to the structures of these groupings in which our laypersons live. This phase of the lay ministry we find particularly difficult. A serious effort is now being made at this point and, as one of the primary emphases in our training program, has brought with it new eagerness and a sense of expectancy.

Again, this life—koinonia and diakonia—can never be adequately described. One can tell only how it breaks forth and the forms and structures which contain and channel it. But the structures are forever changing. New wineskins are constantly being granted to hold new wines. Most important for members is the ability to distinguish between the life itself and the structures which express it.

In a way, belonging to this community does take one out of the world by giving a sense of community which transcends the fragmentation of life in the world.

I am not here trying to deal with the very difficult question of just when a person belongs to the Body of Christ. A Body which visibly shows forth the characteristic marks of the church is basic to evangelism. I believe God wills that every person will come in time to an awareness of the nature of the Body and will share consciously the joy of sin forgiven and the wonder of belonging to a grace community of which Christ is Lord. I believe that the faithful preaching of the Word, the administering of holy communion, and the constant nurturing of those placed in our care are the instruments of God in giving this quality of life. If life in another dimension is not breaking out around us, if lives are not being radically transformed, and if a new community which has redeeming power is not emerging, we must consider the possibility that we are not being faithful to our call.

∿ *The Gifts of the Ministries* ∿

Each person is called to ministry. The ministries will vary. But when God calls a person to belong to God and to God's people, the person is given gifts for the upbuilding of that people and for its ministry to the world. Though there are differing functions, one function is not more essential to the life of the Body than another. Each function is valid and significant and essential to the healthy functioning of the whole, and engagement in the fulfilling of any one function may not be limited to any one individual.

Although certain special functions may be the primary thrust of one person's ministry, this does not mean that those functions are limited to that one person. For example, the primary thrust of a clergyman's calling may well be the ministry of the Word through preaching and teaching, the administering of Holy Communion and the pastoral functions, but this does not mean that only the ordained minister does these things. There is no reason why certain laypersons cannot share in this ministry, not merely as the pastor's arms but as a fulfillment of their own calling. Some lay ministers are greatly gifted in the spiritual nurture of others. In our own congregation, with few exceptions, each member has a little flock or congregation for which he or she is peculiarly responsible. If it is assumed that one pastor will nurture all the members, the depth of the life together will be severely limited. In our conception each member has the joy and responsibility of ministering to other members in the Body.

Perhaps the central thrust of most lay ministers will be in the areas of the world's life. However, the professional minister should not be excluded from this type of activity, for his ministry will be enriched by some costly involvement in the secular.

The principle of balance can help us from centering exclusively on our own special concerns. Each member should in some degree be engaged in a ministry both to the Body and to the world, though the emphasis or major thrust may vary greatly depending upon the call of God and the special gifts the member has been given. This principle of balance could well be applied to the life of the entire congregation to determine whether its life, oriented toward the world, is at the same time adequately shepherding the inner growth of its members.

∾ *Value of the Various Ministries* ∾

One order of ministry is not eternally more valuable than another. To emphasize the significance of one type of ministry could result in making many feel that they are second-class members of the Body, important only as extensions of the official clergy. One psychological reason for this may be that the minister, needing to be the center of a revolving constellation, is unable to be one among a number of equally significant ministers, finding it difficult to decrease while another increases. On the other hand, the layperson may not really want the responsibility involved in ordination as a lay minister of Christ and his church in an industrial society.

One of the most exciting things I have discovered during the past ten years is just this possibility of ministry on the part of every person. Sometimes it takes years of intelligent loving and prayer for this ministry to unfold. But with patience the most wonderful things emerge from the most unpromising people.

There are several areas in which we need concentration of thought and effort if we are to be ready for the new thing which God is eager to do in our midst.

∼ *The Church as a Servant People* ∼

Of greatest importance is our own attitude. The new life of God breaks out most vigorously among new people. There are substructures of our own lives (as professional ministers) that are waiting to be wholly converted. I see us as being the central problem. We ourselves are not convincing in our witness. A greater degree of self-knowledge is necessary. Why do we do what we do? What are our motives? To what degree do we function on the basis of these categories:

  a. doing that which is in keeping with the moral tone of our group;
  b. doing that which gets the desired outcome;
  c. doing that which will please an absentee trustee of our spiritual values;
  d. doing that which will stand up under analysis and logic.

Is our authority really from God or are we bound in the foregoing ways? Do we believe that the people in our congregation are as vital to the life of the Body as we are? Do we give lip service to the concept of the ministry of all believers while being seriously threatened when those ministries begin to emerge? These are not merely academic questions. Real threat is experienced as the circle of activities in which we excel gets smaller and smaller. Unless we see the ministry of the layperson in the world to be of as great a significance as ours, we shall ever be tempted to use him or her as a lackey in our personal fulfillment.

The use of the terms *clergy* and *laity* in our country tends to perpetu-ate the feeling of a second-class order in the church. Many still feel that the clergy carries on the real business of the church and the incidental activities are delegated to the laity. Either a new terminology must be found or the old must be invested with new meaning. How should we designate the full-time ministry of each person called to the laos [people] of God? Although it is not adequately descriptive, in our congregation we speak of the professional minister and the nonprofessional minister. The value of this lies in each member's eventual acceptance of status as a minister, usually having the primary thrust of that ministry in the world. The acceptance of this responsibility often takes time, because old patterns of thinking are strong. But it is thrilling when it comes.

The ordination of a layperson to a ministry in the world is much more than recognition of significant activity. It means that the person knows himself or herself to be grasped by God for a task that he or she can do and that the church must have done. This awareness of God's call has grown out of searching and prayer and participation in various areas of the world's life. Ordination signifies that the individual's sense of call is confirmed by his or her own Christian community. We try to be as specific as possible in defining the layperson's specialized ministry. It is easy to escape responsibility in high-sounding general concepts. The world is a big place and its structures are tough and resistant to Christian penetration. The lay minister seeks to discover just where to exercise obedience. This specialized ministry, though extremely important in our thinking, is conceived to be flexible and may have quite different emphases at different periods of life.

The structures of the church must be geared to implementing this conception. Newness will not emerge because we are eager for it to happen. Nor will it come because we preach on the ministry of all believers. These ministries will emerge when the whole congregation is engaging in its ministry in the world and when the whole structure of the congregational life expresses this intention. When the structures thus express such an aim, a person in his or her first encounter with the church will sense that the church exists as a servant in the world. Such persons may resist the church, and well they might, for they become aware that it is a servant people and they may be unwilling to become a part of it.

∾ Progression of Spiritual Growth ∾

Now a word on our strategy of evangelism. There is a definite progression of experience through which a person is led:

The church exists in the scattered life of the world and, through the witness of its lay ministers, carries on a constant dialogue with the world. There comes a time when the Christian is asked the reason for the hope that is within him or her. This may be the time when it is right to encourage the non-Christian to touch the life of the Christian fellowship. He is left free to explore it at his own pace—to test its reality as he will. The very richness and fullness of the common life in Christ among the believers point up a whole new dimension and speak to deep needs of the nonbeliever. This is true in spite of the fact that intimate contact reveals glaring weaknesses in the Christian fellowship which at a distance might have remained undiscovered. The central factor at this stage is the irresistible charismatic quality of the Christian fellowship when Christ is present. The seeker is often aware that there is a secret at the heart of this people which she does not understand. What is it? The time comes when she wants to know badly enough to make a response.

The next phase is participation in one of the groups of the church, composed of vastly dissimilar persons. In this laboratory of love the seeker learns to worship, pray, study, belong, and perhaps become more deeply involved with other people than ever before in her life. She is introduced to Christian doctrine, ethics, the disciplines of the Christian life, and the drama of the Old and New Testaments. During this period many erroneous concepts are destroyed. This is especially important in a culture which often equates Christianity with the American way of life. We hope that in this period of from nine to eighteen months conversion will occur. If it does:

Through participation in a vocational seminar, a person comes to grips with the issues with which we are grappling here. Experience of the disciplines of prayer and openness to the insights of the group bring about the personal discovery of a special vocation.

The seeker then moves into a small mission group which lives by a simple discipline. The task is to identify and confront an area of the group's specific concern. These missions are meant to be flexible and may change at any time in obedience to God's leading.

I have described something of the present structure of our fellowship. It may have changed by the time I return home. One of our members recently wrote:

> One does not have to be long in the fellowship of this church to
> know that its structures do not last. This has been difficult for

some of us. We have found it hard to part with old forms and ways as though they meant life itself, and indeed this is what we did believe.

Within these walls we have discovered that our days had meaning and we did not yet know the reason of it. In our unknowing we guessed the life we had stumbled upon was dependent upon this person or upon that person or in the ways the classes were scheduled or the groups formed. When the pattern was changed we were shaken by it. It seemed like extreme folly to tamper with what was obviously of God.

The members of the church assured us, counseled with us, comforted us, but they changed the forms as though they had not heard us, and we who had no faith in what was to come grieved for that which had been so newly found and so quickly lost.

Somehow, having endured the times of change, we discovered that the life of the church does not rest in its structures. We learned with the ever-changing programs that the organization and institutional forms were important only because the life they held was important. This life was unpredictable, breaking out anew in unexpected places and in unexpected ways. The structures were to hold it as wineskins are to hold wine. As new life broke in, new structures were needed.

∾ New Wineskins ∾

I believe the primary task of the professional is to train nonprofessional ministers for their ministry. The professional will prepare nonprofessional ministers to grapple with the implications of rapid social change in their fields of specialized ministry. The laity's task is much more difficult than ours, because it is not as safe.

This training will require a focused ministry. We cannot do this in addition to all the things we are accustomed to doing. We cannot do this and fulfill the traditional roles expected of us by our people. This type of ministry will involve misunderstanding, pressure, and, at times, hostility. But, of all people, we should understand hostility and expect it. When they say all manner of evil against us, we should not wonder, as if some strange thing were happening to us. Perhaps this focused ministry will seem like a narrowing of our ministries. I believe the opposite to be true. I believe this to be the fastest way of winning the masses to Christ and penetrating the structures which mold their lives.

Part III

~⁓~

Living Together in Christ

5

The Way to Life

~

In 1959, thirteen years after its founding, the congregation of The Church of the Saviour grappled with the process of becoming a follower of Christ and living a life of devotion and faithfulness.

A passage from the eleventh chapter of Matthew (11:28) says that the way is easy. But a passage from the seventh chapter of Matthew (7:13) says that the way is hard. When we say that truth is paradoxical, we are saying that it is contradictory. What we eventually come to know is that life is not nearly as simple as we thought, and there are different dimensions of almost every issue. We come to see that the New Testament, which gives us the original documents of our faith, is realistic. It deals with various dimensions of life, and life is complex. In one sense the Christian gospel is very easy. The easiest thing in the world is to give one's heart to Jesus Christ, to love him, to follow him, to know that fullness and ecstasy of life which come through him. But there is also a sense in which the Christian life is just about the most difficult thing that anybody ever conceived. It's hard to be a Christian; this is obvious, because there are so few of them. A genuine, radiant, spontaneous, transmitting Christian is a rare commodity.

G. K. Chesterton said that Christianity "has not been tried and found wanting; it has been found difficult and left untried."[1] I think this is close to the truth. Jesus said:

> "Enter by the narrow gate; for the gate is wide and the way is easy, that leads to destruction, and those who enter by it are many. For the gate is narrow and the way is hard, that leads to life, and those who find it are few." (Matt. 7:13–14, RSV)

Something within me, something within you finds this Christian way of life (when we take it seriously) difficult. There are some points for stumbling. Paul talks about Christianity's being a scandal. Emil Brunner has written a little book entitled, *The Scandal of Christianity.* Certainly we often stumble when we think seriously about the Christian faith.

Let us consider several things inherent within the Christian faith which make it very difficult to be a Christian:

The theological assumptions upon which we, as Christians, build our lives are very difficult. I am aware that many people in this country believe in God. All you have to do is check the various censuses to find that almost everybody does. There is a lot of piety along the Potomac and along all the rivers and highways. To believe in God is easy. To believe in the God and Father of our Lord Jesus Christ is quite different. The difficult assumptions have to do with:

a. *The Christian doctrine of God.* Christian faith is understood to grow out of a real encounter in which something happens that cannot happen solely within a person's thought life. A very real encounter takes place with a God who is self-revealing, a God who is self-operating and self-affirming and self-disclosing, a God who enters history as the Living Lord. This God cannot be devised in human thinking. God is always the absolute subject and can never become our object. God can be discovered only through God's own self-disclosure. This God knows an unconditional sovereignty and freedom which constitute an affront to us. To believe in such a God is a scandal. But this is the God the Old and New Testaments portray.

b. *The Christian concept of humanity* also seems to be an affront to almost everyone, to modern people as well as to those who lived in the past. Christianity says that we are creatures. We are not God. We have been created by, and are entirely dependent upon God. God says, "I am the Lord, and there is no other, besides me there is no God" (Isa. 45:5, *RSV*).

That we are special creatures is certainly true. We alone are created in such a way that we can receive God's Word and can live in communion with God. We are the creatures God can talk to, and we can and must reply. A definite answer is expected of us. The Christian faith says, however, that the very essence of our humanity has been violated, that we are in reality living in contradiction to the will of God, to our own destiny, and to our own beings.

The problem is that we may decide that our freedom, which is grounded in responsibility, is too limited. Instead of being free in God, we want to be free from God. We want to be our own God. We desire to break down the barriers of creaturely, relative freedom and to substitute for it a divine, absolute freedom. By this attempt to emancipate ourselves from dependence on the divine, we entangle ourselves in a desperate, incurable contradiction of our own being. Being free within God, we become slaves by denying our dependence on God.

Thus our status before God is changed. We are guilty, and our guilt means that we are separated from God. This situation comes to be beyond our own control. In the midst of our need and our powerlessness, we are lost from God; we are cut off from God. Into this situation God must enter. God must effect the reconciliation. God can and does bridge this chasm—in his son, our savior, Jesus Christ. God brings forgiveness by the atoning death of Jesus Christ.

One can see immediately that this is a very difficult truth. This is shattering to one's very selfhood—not to the creative, true self, but to the false self we ordinarily call the ego. If we accept the truth of our reconciliation through the death of Jesus Christ, then everything has to change. We are no longer our own persons. We are hopelessly indebted. We are no longer in a position to call the moves. Someone else is calling them, someone else is in control. It is doubtful that we ever like this. Christianity is difficult because this is the God it knows and this is its position concerning human beings. The doctrine is that only God can come into the situation, bridge the chasm, and heal the brokenness and the estrangement.

c. *We are asked to follow and to surrender our wills to God when we cannot predict what God is going to do.* We know that we must be on our way, that we must be on the move. But we cannot know just exactly where we are going because that depends upon the living will of this Other. And although God is immutable, God is mystery as far as we are concerned. The human, finite mind can never with certainty predict what God is going to do. "For my thoughts are not your thoughts, neither are your ways my ways, says the Lord" (Isa. 55:8, *RSV*). In one sense we know less and less about God and God's ways with us. We are less and less able to predict what this living, sovereign, free God is going to do in any moment of history. Nevertheless, if the Christian faith is real, we must put ourselves into the hands of this God without reserve, with glorious abandon. We must sing, "Where he leads me I will follow; I'll go with him all the way," not knowing where we're going. And I submit to you that this is not easy.

d. The Christian faith always involves *a movement from self to God*. Anything else is a perversion. We tend to make Christianity a creed to hold or an ethic to live by. But these are not the central things. They are comparatively easy. The real challenge is a progressive dying to one's self, a progressive integrating around Christ. We must come to the place where we can say, "I have been crucified with Christ; it is no longer I who live, but Christ who lives in me" (Gal. 2:20, *RSV*). I believe it is impossible to overstate the radical nature of this change, the pain of it, the desolation of it at times. But integration around self is a perversion of our real natures. It spells insanity and death. To the degree that we are in Christ and he in us, we are whole and that spells fullness and, at times, even ecstasy.

Consideration of this movement from self to God leads to certain observations:

• We are impotent to initiate the movement. We can respond to the movement of God, but we cannot initiate it. Confessing our helplessness and our need, our brokenness and our sin can open a sterile life to a regenerating tide—can let Christ be born in us. But our part is only reception, surrender, yielding; and then comes the expression. God is the one who does the converting. When we believe ourselves successful in reforming ourselves by willpower and self-cultivation in Christian thinking we fail. Self-improvement is of no avail because, as the Christian knows, the very self must die.

So the first observation is that we cannot initiate the movement. Only God can do that. We can respond to it.

• The start of the movement from self to God—when we respond to God and God's work in us begins in earnest—is usually painful. It may be that we have already been living in so much pain that the pain of this dying is even a relief. However, because it is seldom easy to put anything before one's self, there is always an element of pain when we begin this Christian life in earnest.

Holding on to ourselves is really ridiculous, especially when we examine the pathetic self that we hold on to. One mistake is to think it is easier to give oneself away if one does not possess much. I worked unsuccessfully for months with a man whose wife and children had left him and no longer cared about him. He stumbled from one third-rate hotel to another. He looked out at life through a continual alcoholic haze. He had no money, no creative work, no position, no prestige, no status. Yet even this sad creature could not give himself away. Finally, in abject misery and despair, he died a suicide's death.

Never a matter of whether we have much or little, we always try to hold on to ourselves. We have our pride. We find it very difficult to say, "Father, I have sinned. I am helpless. I cannot do it. I am utterly dependent on you." God must be first, with no other concern of life taking precedence. If family comes first, that is idolatry; it is to commit suicide. If business and success and security take a priority over God, that is idolatry; that is to die. Perhaps the reason the doctrine of our church seems hard at times is because, in the name of Christ, we keep insisting on the death of the self—insisting on the continuing movement from self to God. And the ego screams. We try not to let up during this process even when we would much prefer not to witness the operation. This emphasis means that we shall lose some people that we want very much to keep. But we cannot accept them in the name of Christ unless he is in truth their sovereign Master and Lord. We are seeking to let God produce a group of holy people in the best sense of that word, wholly devoted to God.

The second observation is that, when we begin this Christian way in earnest, there is an element of pain because the self begins to die and Christ begins to be all-in-all, until one day we shall really be able to say, "My Lord and my God! It is no longer I who live but Christ who lives in me."

• During the process of the movement from self to God, the soul makes a subtle shift. The initial, genuine start has been made. The light has finally broken on our understanding. Flesh and blood have not revealed this to us; God has given us this revelation. At last we confess to him. At last we believe. At last the encounter has occurred. We sigh in relief. We feel that finally the self is dead.

But exactly what has happened? The self has made a subtle shift, no longer holding God off by arguments of the mind. Christian theology is seen now to be truth. However, the self is not yet ready to surrender completely. Having become familiar with religious jargon, a new vocabulary, the self now talks glibly about the prayer of relinquishment, surrender, yielding. After about two months at The Church of the Saviour a person can fling the words around without any trouble at all. He can identify himself with almost anybody he talks to. She has the time of her life promenading around in religious garments. The self has made a subtle shift.

Some of the familiar stages of this journey are described by a woman named Emily Herman in her book entitled *Creative Prayer*:

> At the beginning of our prayer life we are self-centered. Prayer means little more to us than asking. We ask for personal favors, for blessings upon ourselves and those belonging to us. In our prayer vocabulary personal pronouns occupy a disproportionate place. It is my needs, my relations, my friends; and even when we go further afield and pray for those whom we have never seen, it is because their needs have been so presented to us as to stir our sympathies and appeal to our idiosyncrasies. In the last resort we still make use of God in prayer. . . . There comes a time when this kind of prayer no longer suffices . . . We feel the stirring of that buried life in the deeps below consciousness."[2]

This marks the next move. At first this may "lead to nothing more than a revolt against institutional religion." You can watch this phase in a person's life. "We feel unsatisfied with what churches and religious systems have to offer. . . . The remedies they possess do not touch the aching nerve of our being. At this stage we shall be tempted to turn from organized forms . . . of the corporate Body of Christ" that repel us and seek refuge "in the solitude of our own spirits."

But let us remember that "the soul that finds nothing but emptiness within the collective experience and life of believers will find nothing but hallucination and delusion within its solitary self." It is in this stage that

> we are conscious of restlessness, dissatisfaction, peevishness. The house of selfhood is being demolished over our heads. What satisfied us before inspires us now with weariness and distaste. The shell of natural religiousness has cracked and our unloveliness obtrudes. . . . It is a period of baneful incubation. . . . A demand is being made upon us—the demand for obedience.
>
> Then, perhaps by a sudden, sharp invasion of a new life flooding ours from without . . . or by the sudden rising of the flood from within the depths of the spirit—probably by the meeting of both—we become conscious of the birth of the Christ-spirit within ourselves, and of our own birth into a new and wonderful world. Or the process may be of the most gentle and almost imperceptible nature. A brooding stillness about us, the coming of light we know not how. . . . But however it

comes, it means the soul's emergence into a world familiar yet almost frighteningly unfamiliar—a world in which we feel utterly strange and awkward, and which we yet recognize as our true home.

We've known all along we ought to have lived here. And so we are now in a whole new world, a new world of values, of untold beauties, of deathless hope. "We have become dead to a whole universe of delights and sorrows, and alive to an entirely different range of thoughts and emotions."

This mode of life is all so new, so entrancing. We cannot get enough of it and we go around talking to everybody about it. I'm grateful for this. I feel outrage when I hear a person put the damper upon another by saying, "This is only the honeymoon stage; you will get over it." What a cruel thing to do! Yes, he or she will get over it but should enjoy this phase and the meaning of it—this new world never known before.

Now what happens? The self, not yet dead, has merely lost consciousness of its existence for a season. In its absorption in a new object of desire the self now clings to its spiritual treasures as it once clung to the goods of earth. Only when God withdraws these spiritual possessions from us do we realize how largely self-centered we have been in holding on to them. And one by one God usually takes them from us.

The tendency all along has been for the self, dressed up in its religious clothes, to use God. God is to sanction our plans, which, of course, are for God. God is to give us peace and joy in order that we may use this peace and joy, for God, of course. But we find ourselves making use of the most majestic and ultimate power in life. If we can do this without being aware of it, then we are truly bound up in ourselves. In this way so many supposedly religious people are unattractive. They are using God instead of letting God use them. Such persons are going to be tense and irritable. Because of our tendency to use God, God must strip us so that we can love God for who God is.

Each stage is fraught with danger. For this reason we must surrender at each succeeding level of life. Gifts are granted to us and new strengths come. Sometimes it is more difficult to give God our new strengths than it was to give up our old brokenness. So, in addition to giving ourselves to God daily, denying ourselves, and taking up our cross and following Christ, we must, after careful preparation, give to God in an act of decisive commitment each new phase of life:

- the new business
- the new job
- getting out of debt
- deliverance from a habit
- the engagement, the marriage, the coming of the baby
- new friends
- new insights
- new popularity and power
- new projects into which we enter.

All of these should be given to God in a clear and specific act of surrender, because the question is, can we handle these new gifts? So often we can't. Then, as we learn to surrender moment by moment, day by day, week by week, and month by month, the time will come when the self as we knew it no longer exists. We have really become "new creations in Christ Jesus," with the power to transmit his life, with the power of his radiance, with the power of his beauty, with the power to heal and to bring people back from estrangement into the presence of the atoning Christ.

If you really want to travel along this pilgrim way, you must recognize that this is a lifetime task, and no mean task, with no shortcuts. Don't start unless you intend to stay with it. To begin and then try to stop in the middle is foolhardy. Jesus warned us about this. If you try to start and then stop, you are neither fish nor fowl, neither man nor beast, neither sinner nor saint. The strain will tear you to pieces. A decision made in one's soul changes the whole course of life. A destiny is formed. God is calling you through his son Jesus Christ, our Lord and Savior. Is there a stirring in your soul? God is reaching out to you. Will you reach out to God?

Notes

[1] *Collected Works of G. K. Chesterton,* vol. 4: *What's Wrong with the World* (San Francisco: Ignatius Press, 1986), pt.1, chap. 5.

[2] Emily Herman, *Creative Prayer* (New York and London: Harper & Brothers, 1934), pp. 87, 92–93. The following quotations are from pages 92–95.

6

Oneness

~

In 1956 Gordon explored the issues of reconciliation and the process of becoming the Body of Christ.

There is a malady which is ours simply because we are human beings. Having come to know the sickness, we seek to look at the answer which God has given in Christ and why it is that God's answer is the only answer to that particular disease which is ours. The grace of God continues to be mediated into our lives so that we shall continue to be free, continue to know the delirious joy of the constant love of God and of God's continuing forgiveness.

We are brought into the accepting community by what we call reconciliation or justification. This is the greatest experience which can happen in human life. As we enter into this experience, we also enter into a relationship with one another. For the Christian this is the very ground of existence; this is the most important thing that has ever occurred in life; this is more important than anything that will occur in the future.

When people tell us, "There are certain things which you must face; you must be realistic; you must be honest," we say, "Yes, but the first thing we must be realistic about is this tremendous thing which has occurred in our lives. God has actually met us; we have entered a relationship with him; we belong to him." We can say, "I know whom I have believed and am persuaded that he is able to keep that which I have committed unto him against that day" (2 Tim. 1:12, *KJV*). And this is a note of triumph; this is a note of joy.

If there is an interim period of suffering in the meantime, we know that glory is going to be revealed in us at the last time and God is going to complete that which he has begun. We believe this to be realism. We do not believe this to be whistling in the dark. We believe that it was realism when Jesus was talking to his disciples, all of whom were going to desert him just a few hours later, and he himself was going to die upon a cross. And he said to them, "Be of good cheer, I have overcome the world" (John 16:33, *RSV*). That breaks your heart because of the sheer audacity, the courage of it, with all of his disciples believing him. He could die a death upon the cross and say, "Cheer up, I have overcome the world."

So it is with Christians. We say, "That's all right, there are a lot of interim problems, a lot of difficulties. There are a lot of things concerning which we will be realistic, to be sure. But we can afford to cheer up, because Christ has overcome the world and we belong to him in his own Body, which is the accepted and the accepting community."

The Christian community is not only to be the accepting community; it is to go past the point of simply accepting people where they are. It is to go to the point where it knows a oneness within its life, akin to the life which Christ knew because God was perfectly in him and he was perfectly in God. The Body of the Lord Jesus Christ is essentially one. We have the freedom to violate the essential nature of the Body, to rip it apart and to cause it to be in schism. But the Body is essentially one body.

Jesus was aware of our freedom, aware how often we would misuse it. He was aware that unless there were this oneness, the world would never really believe him. Therefore, the burden of his prayer is: "God, hold them together. Everything in the world will tend to pull them apart. They will get opposition from without. False prophets will come; false teachers will come. They are not of the world; the world will hate them because they are not of it. And worse than anything else, there will be problems arising from within themselves which will be much more difficult than the opposition from without. So God, please hold them together that they may be perfectly one even as we are one."

The world will never believe that God has broken into our life until others become aware of this divine oneness. The world will never believe that God has actually sent his Christ until it sees his Body functioning with this sort of unity.

Now this oneness is not uniformity. With so much uniformity and conformity in today's world, we tend to fear that to become deeply

Christian will be to give ourselves to the sort of uniformity which we rightly resist.

Sadly, uniqueness and individuality are deteriorating. That which produces conformity is sin. That which produces uniqueness and difference is Christian faith. When, in order to grow, you give yourself utterly to God in Christ and to the Christian fellowship, you are freed so that your own distinctiveness and uniqueness can at last come to birth. This is important. No uniformity is demanded. Conformity is quite different from what we mean when we speak of unity.

Nor are we talking about submissiveness, either to God or to a group. Some of us may feel, "Well, I don't know anything else to do with my life. God seems to always have his way in the end. He is bigger than I am. Why keep fighting it? I might as well submit. I've been bruised and battered enough." Or a person may long for a vital life in intimate relationships with other people. "Okay, here's a group that will accept me as I am. I might as well do whatever they say I must do in order to belong. If they've got a commitment and a few disciplines, I suppose I'd better try to enter into the commitment and the disciplines too." But this is submission. This is another form of tyranny. This is not the way of Christian faith.

Christian faith involves a glad, joyful self-surrender. An awareness has dawned that the most wonderful thing in the world is simply, with all the stops out, to give one's life to a loving God. We are so grateful that God is there that we are overwhelmed. The gratitude tends to warm our hearts—gratitude for having been led to a group of people through whom this grace can be mediated. What else can I do except give myself fully to these people? This is the Body of Christ!

Submissiveness is markedly different from joyful self-surrender as conformity is different from oneness.

In order to be instruments of God for oneness, we must learn to recognize the practices that tear down oneness. We will do well to remember that any sin cuts one off from fellowship with God and with other people. Any sin.

Sometimes we say, "I just can't feel close to those people." There may be a lot of reasons why you can't feel close to people. Sin, whether it is a sin of commission or a sin of omission, will make you feel isolated and lonely—will keep you from feeling the togetherness and the oneness. Sin, in the last analysis, is separation, self-idolatry—a refusal to accept the true ground of our being, which is God. When we set ourselves up as the ground of our own existence we are simply in rebellion against things as they are. Rebellion against God is ultimately death for ourselves and death for other people. The only way sin can ever be healed is at the cost of a cross, and God himself must go to this cross. He must bear it within his own heart. So Christians never take any form of sin lightly. We ought never to condone it because we always have a terrific stake in it ourselves. Whenever any person sins I am hurt. And whenever I sin others are hurt. We are bound together. None of us lives alone. We are tied up in an organic relationship of humanity first, and then, in a special way, within the Christian fellow-ship. But sin always produces isolation and loneliness.

One particular form of sin which hurts this delicate fabric of oneness which Christ is trying to produce is the matter of talk. If you listen sometimes to the talk that goes on, day after day and night after night, you will come to be aware of the hidden hostility and resentment being verbalized. "The tongue . . . is an unruly evil, full of deadly poison" (James 3:8, *KJV*), said James, and how well he knew!

Often a conversation begins, "I shouldn't say this, but . . . " Of course, our answer as Christians should be, "Well, if you shouldn't say it, don't." But we think, "Well, let's hear this juicy morsel." Then we try to do something to retrieve it after we've learned what it is. Christians should always be careful about saying anything that may drive any kind of wedge between people, because such wedges will produce loneli-ness.

Someone may say, "Well, he just needs to talk. I'd better listen to him." We do need to talk. But we need to talk in a trusted relationship where we can be helped, where there is someone mature enough to help us, to reflect back to us what we are really saying. Loose talk destroys the very thing we must have to live. We must have unity in the fellowship because we are made for it, but talk can lacerate unity—can cause spiritual suicide.

Another destroyer of oneness—and most of us are good at this—is the irritability we feel because others do not give themselves in just the way we feel they should, considering the maturity we think they should have. They haven't responded in just the way that I feel they should respond. And I'm probably right! But the minute our irritability comes into the picture we cut off any possible helpfulness that we can bring. They need someone to understand them—to give them support and love, so that they can be released enough to let their lives flow into sacrificial channels of service. But we do the very thing which isolates them further, complicates their picture, and makes life more difficult for them.

The problem may be that they have not seen enough genuine joy in the sacrificial service that we've been rendering to feel that they want to get into this business. We don't know how to manufacture that joy, so all we can do is become irritated because they don't get it.

What happens? We set ourselves over against the fellowship. We think, "I've responded properly, but these poor people haven't." So a wedge has been driven within the oneness that Christ intended. Whereas if we could say, "God, there is real need here and I am in need myself. Because of that, I will go to you as I have not gone before and I will undergird these immature people. I will love them and I will pray for them and I will be available in any way that you show me. But help me to love them with the passion with which you love them."

We all need to recognize the dangers to our oneness even when they come through our best friends. This is where we are often tripped up. We think that any difficulty will come through some alien situation, but often it comes through our closest friend. This is what happened to Jesus. When he told Peter he would have to go to the cross, Peter said, "Wait a minute, Lord. Surely you won't do that. That would not be right." Jesus turned, and with as much vehemence as you will find recorded anywhere, he said,"Get thee behind me, Satan, for you do not understand the things which are of God, but the things which are of men" (Mark 8:33, paraphrased). Here was temptation coming through one of the three in the inner circle. Often our problem—tragic divisiveness—comes from a person in our inner circle, perhaps from our best friend.

We have considered some of the dangers. What are some of the things we can do to upbuild the Body of Christ and to let God give us this oneness?

We could spend some time each day speaking about this unity, remembering that we are organically bound to one another. Most of us continue to function as individuals. The closest analogy that I know is that of marriage. People who are really married never make major decisions without remembering that they are organically bound to their partner. For instance, I would be in trouble if somebody invited me to go out to dinner, and I forgot that I am married to Mary. A married person considers his or her spouse in relation to every question that comes up, every decision that has to be made. This is similarly true within the Christian fellowship. We need to be so aware of the fact that we are organically bound to those in the Body of the Lord Jesus Christ that we don't make any major decision without knowing that it affects the whole Body. But this takes a little doing and doesn't come to us overnight.

The second suggestion is that we shall be loyal to that which we agree to as a Body so that we sound a strong, united note of witness for whatever it is we feel God is leading us to be or to do. What does God want us to do as a church? We must discern this as best we can through our individual devotions and in our times of corporate prayer. Then, having corporately made the decision as to where and how God is leading us, we must be loyal to the things we have decided. "If the trumpet give an uncertain sound, who shall prepare himself for the battle?" (1 Cor. 14:8, *KJV*). If any part of the Body of Christ gives forth an uncertain sound; if we don't really know what we are committed to, and we are not loyal to it after we have decided, then no one is going to gird himself for the battle. But we should be excited because the kingdom is dawning and Christ is on the move! We have committed ourselves to a loyalty of action.

We also need a very real loyalty to one another. There is a false loyalty, and there is a wonderful kind of loyalty shown by a husband who loves his wife and a wife who loves her husband. Those of us who are bound together in Christian relationship must stand by one another and interpret one another to those who need that interpretation. We learn to rejoice in the strengths of one another rather than being threatened because of another's strength.

Suppose another person can do a better job of counseling than you can do or ever will do? Wonderful! That helps me—that helps you. Is there a person who can give more liberally than you can? Wonderful! That lifts the whole tone of the Body. Is there a person who can pray for two hours and you can't pray for fifteen minutes? Wonderful! This very thing may enable you to learn to pray. We need the ability actually to rejoice in the strength of another rather than be threatened by it.

Sometimes we try to pull another down to our level because the very fact of that person's soaring threatens us. There are times when we even want others to fail, especially those very strong people. If we can find something weak about one of the strong spirits, this seems to give us a sort of secret satisfaction.

Sometimes we even want the church to fail. We seem to be determined, even though we say that we belong to Christ, to let people know that "we are not carried away as some people are. We've got our feet on the ground." My hope would be that all of us would be carried away. If I understand the Gospel at all, God got carried away over his children. What else could have ever made him come? What else would have ever sent Christ to the cross? I think God intends and expects his children to be carried away. God intends that sometime before we die we shall be able to say wholeheartedly, "At last I know what life is all about. At last I'm able to respond to a love which is the most tremendous thing life has ever known!"

When that happens we are going to be loyal to one another, and also we will not condone the sins of one another. To condone sin is to do a serious injustice to a person. A person may come to us with a problem—perhaps a problem with prayer, saying, "I'm having difficulty. I simply can't pray." We may say, in effect, "I understand this. I'm having trouble myself." Now, this is really to say, "Tut, tut. It doesn't make any difference because, if I'm having trouble, it can't be too serious a thing that you're having trouble too."

The person has come to us in all probability asking one of two things. He has come asking that we relieve the anxiety which has him boxed in. To quell his anxiety, he wants us to say, "Prayer doesn't really make that much difference. This is just the common life. Don't worry too much about it."

Or he is saying, "I want to learn to pray, for this makes all the difference in the world. Will you help me?" But we say, "Tut, tut, it doesn't matter." Now the purpose of life is to come to love Christ and, since one day we shall be in his presence, I don't think that person will thank us for saying that prayer didn't matter. Our loyalty to one another demands that we not condone each other's sins and our weaknesses. We are to help one another in order that these weak places shall be strengthened and our unforgiven areas forgiven.

Also, if we are going to be loyal to one another I suggest that we learn to handle the divisive threats which are always being given to us. One of the devil's most effective weapons is to divide people. If he can get us divided by saying, "This person's leadership is different from another person's leadership," and by suggesting various things that are divisive, then his job is done. We need to learn to recognize these threats and to know how to handle them. Let me give you one illustration:

A person may come to me and say, "You know, I just don't like So-and-So. If this is an example of what Christianity is, if I'm going to have to put up with a person like this, I think I want to call this thing off. Because not only do I not go for this person now, I don't think I'm ever going to go for her." What do you say? You may say, "I don't go for her either. I find it very difficult to be enthusiastic about her. I know what you mean. But we will try to love her." That response threatens the oneness immediately because you are participating in these divisive threats and separating yourself from the family, from the fellowship.

What can you do? You can say this to the person: "You know, So-and-So is a young Christian, just as all of us are. She herself would say that she had not gotten all of these things squared away, and she would be the first to tell you that if you had a chance to have a serious conversation with her. She has a lot of things she's working on. I myself do not know her well enough—I'm not qualified to know where she ought to be at a given moment. But this is what I'd like to say. The strange thing about this Christian fellowship is that it glories in having all sorts and conditions of people at all different stages of development. If you are going to explore the Christian faith within the context of the Christian church and especially this church, you're going to have to come to terms with So-and-So."

These things you can say gently. You haven't glossed over the faults of So-and-So. You've indicated that you're not qualified to judge just how mature or immature this person should be. But you have let the complainer know that, if intending to explore the Christian faith, he or she is going to have to deal with imperfect people. Furthermore, we are sticking together—not out of a false loyalty but because Christ has called us into an experience together. Who in the world am I to exclude a person that Christ has called to belong to his Body? Having used this approach time and again, I believe it to be an effective way of deflecting criticism of another.

One other suggestion for realizing this oneness with the joys that come from it is to learn to take real pride in one another. You say, "How in the world are you going to do that? The better you get to know people, the more you know what they're struggling with. To take pride in these people is to be unrealistic, isn't it?"

Recently I have been reading the seventeenth chapter of John. I'm trying to understand it. In his closing prayer, just a few minutes before the disciples are all going to desert him, and just a few hours after they have been arguing about who was to have first place in his kingdom, Jesus begins to thank God for the gift of his disciples. These weak, foolish, stupid disciples! He says, "God, you have given them to me and I thank you for them." He says, "I am glorified in them." He says, "They are not of the world even as I am not of the world." And he does this, when he knows that they are going to desert him and after they have been fighting for first place in what they considered to be an earthly kingdom. Yet he is saying that beneath it all, they are essentially different from the world. "And God, I thank you that you have given me this group of people to live with and now to die for." This I have difficulty understanding, but this is what he did.

Jesus must be saying that, with his grace, you and I can come to take pride in one another. We can thank God for all the people he has given us through the years—weak, fallible people—not trying to cover over and gloss over their weaknesses. If the Son of God could feel that way about twelve weak, fallible disciples, surely we who are human, having our hearts warmed by his love, can begin to take pride in one another because he has given us one another.

If these things we will see and begin to do, he will come himself and with his wondrous love and power he will make us one. And the world will believe as it has never believed before that he did come and that he is available now to cure its deep sickness and meet its great need.

7

Discipline of Love

~

*In this 1956 homily Gordon addresses the necessity of forgiveness
and love in the journey toward wholeness.*

Christian growth is a movement from self to God; it is a progressive
growing into a communion with God, into a friendship with God, until
we come to the place where we are aware of God's presence.

That which hinders us from knowing the reality of his presence is
ourselves, our own lack of openness, our own unwillingness to belong
totally to another—our resistance to the One who claims us totally for
himself.

The ego is the self which hinders us from this friendship, this
communion. Growth is a necessity for our very beings, as there is no
such thing as a static human personality. Either we are progressing, or
we are in a time of retrogression. Scripture commands that we grow
into the fullness of the stature of Christ.

Growth always involves suffering; it does not happen spontaneously.
People do not just naturally grow into great Christians. They grow as
they make certain ordered responses to life.

These ordered responses are called *disciplines*. To be helpful a
discipline needs to be balanced, relating us properly to the three great
areas of life: God, people, and things. Also, a discipline must be
specific, because we are prone to generalize. Further, if we adopt a
discipline, we should at the same time take steps to see how we have
lived, judged by this discipline which we have accepted. We should not
adopt a discipline until we are willing to be reflective concerning it—to
check ourselves against it. To fail to do this is to become unreal,

dishonest people. We may feel that we are doing that which we are, in fact, not doing.

In Christian thinking, in order to grow into the fullness of the stature of Christ, one primary discipline is essential. This discipline is clearly stated in the words of Jesus: "Love one another even as I have loved you" (John 13:34, RSV). There is genius in the way those words are phrased. We immediately want to shout, "Now wait a minute! Is this really necessary? Can't I get close to God without getting involved with people?"

A few weeks ago a young man came to me and said, "I am in great need, and I am aware of it. I need help. There is one thing I would like to get straight with you though before I start. I don't want to get involved with any people. I never have felt comfortable with people, and I don't feel especially comfortable with the people of the church. Now, will you help me?"

When we are confronted by, and respond to God, the Father/ Mother of our Lord Jesus Christ, by virtue of our response we are brought into new relations with people. We become a part of a new community. This is an inevitable part of the response to God.

These are two aspects of the same thing, and they are never separated in Scripture. "You shall love the Lord your God with all your heart, and with all your soul, and with all your mind . . . [and] your neighbor as yourself" (Matt. 22:37–39, *RSV*).

To say that we love God and not to let this love affect our relationships with people is to love God in a speculative fashion. In such a way a man may say: "I love my wife—get that straight—but I do not care about the things she cares about. I am not concerned about the people she's concerned about. I do not care about the hurts which she feels. I'm not interested in her integrity as a person. I do not care about her destiny, her eternal destiny with God. I do not care about these things, but please know that I love her!" These are mere words. To say that we love God and not be concerned about people is to have made an idol of our own thought of God.

Everything we know from the Christian revelation tells us that there is a God behind the universe who cares for us. We are very deeply loved. This is one of the inexhaustible meanings of Calvary: God loves us to the death; God loves us beyond death. For me to say that I love God and do not care about the people who are carried on God's heart, and for whom he died, is not to love God at all.

To enter into the love of God is to begin to carry many people on one's heart. These things are so closely tied together in Scripture that to have a ruptured human relationship is to have a ruptured relationship with God. Jesus was talking about this when he said, "When you come to the chapel on Sunday morning and you are getting ready to offer your gift at the altar, if you remember that your brother has anything against you, and if there is anything you can do to heal that relationship, hold your gift, get your relationship straight, then come back and worship me, because I am the God who is interested in that person with whom you have a ruptured relationship" (Matt. 5:23–24, *RSV*, paraphrased).

Paul says, "Owe no one anything, except to love one another; for he who loves his neighbor has fulfilled the law"(Rom. 13:8, RSV).

The word *love* is misunderstood. It is used promiscuously; it can mean almost anything, can't it? But in the Christian sense it has a precise meaning. Four aspects of that precise meaning of the word love are:

First—Christian love perceives another as a person created in God's image—as a unique bit of God's fashioning God has a stake in every person in the world. Every vulnerable person is made in God's image, and for one person to wander outside the fold of God's concern and caring is to bring an ache to the heart of God. God is the infinite shepherd who yearns over the children stamped with his own image.

This is quite a thought—that God is willing to be vulnerable, to suffer over every child who does not enter into close fellowship and communion with God. This is where we start in this business of Christian love: every person is of priceless value, because a bit of God's very self has entered into him or her. God has entered into this creation, and not to see every human being as God's creation is to see one another for less than we are. Jesus used harsh language on this subject when, in the Sermon on the Mount, he said, "Whoever calls his brother a fool shall be in danger of hell fire!" (Matt. 5:22, *RSV*, paraphrased).

We say, "Well, there's nothing to that. I call my brother a fool every day." And, of course, we do. But Jesus says that, in doing this, we are in eternal jeopardy. Why? His response might be, "Because I have stamped my image on every human being. I have a destiny for every human being, and for you not to see *any* person as one with unique capacities is for you to be guilty of the sin of contempt—to be guilty of the murder of the soul, which is as bad as murder of the body."

With an attitude of contempt toward another you make it difficult for that person to respect herself; you make it difficult for her to find her own identity as a person. Sometimes, of course, in crude terms, we write off a whole group of people or a whole race in one single word. This is the sin of contempt.

We have our more subtle ways of asserting our superiority and making it difficult for others to find themselves as persons under God. Sometimes we say that we just love people for "themselves." Now this is to say nothing. Who are these persons? Bits of protoplasm? Groups of chemicals? Then to love them for their own sake is to love them for a bunch of protoplasm. But the Christian faith says we are to love a person for Christ's sake—not for his or her own sake. Our value has to be derived from something; it has to be rooted somewhere; our value is rooted in the God who made us, who cares for us eternally, and who died for us.

This is the first part of what it means to love: to see a person as one made in the image of God, yearned over by God, able to respond to God, a person who will know an eternal destiny in God.

Second—a Christian loves another person irrespective of any merit he or she may have. No one ever deserves love. We did not, nor do we now deserve the love with which we have been loved. Therefore, we have no right to expect another person to deserve the love which we deign to give him or her.

Love *creates* value rather than demanding it. Unfortunately, what ordinarily happens is that we demand value. Christian love creates value by loving; whether or not a person merits our love has nothing to do with whether he in turn loves. Don't think this is an easy fact to accept, because to begin really to see it is to feel that it is almost immoral. For you say, "I have no right to do that. For me to keep loving people who don't make any response, who don't live up to what they ought to live up to, is to weaken them. It is immoral."

But we are to give this love, whether we are emotionally drawn to a person or whether we are repelled. You know people you just don't like. There seems to be something in the atmosphere; before they get to you the atmosphere seems to press in around you. Yet those people who are so very hard to love and who repel us are the very persons who need us most.

We say, "Well, if that is the way he is going to be, I just won't bother with him. Who is *ever* going to love through all the weirdness of this person? Why should I endure my own Calvary along with Christ to win that person?" When a person is unattractive, when a person is weird, he is trying in all his false ways to maintain his own integrity as a person. He is trying to maintain his identity, trying to be himself. Or it may be that the only way that she can get attention is to be obnoxious. She would rather have people hate her than not know she's around. The more difficult a person is to love, the more that person needs to be loved.

There is a half-truth, however, which I want to point out in this connection. Sometimes we say that we do not have to like a person, we have to love him or her. And that is true with certain reservations. When we say that, we are usually using it as an excuse not to get too deeply involved with someone. We intend to love with kid gloves on. We are going to love and keep our distance. "I'm not sure I really like this person. I will simply direct toward her my undiscourageable goodwill—but I will keep my distance!"

Yet to become involved in the life of another, really to give one's self totally to the other, is to come to the place very soon where we will be emotionally drawn to that person. We will get behind the person's protective armor and begin to experience a warm, emotional feeling. This surprises me about myself. I love a lot of people now in a very deep emotional way although just a year or so ago I knew I could never love them. But I became involved with them. I began to see their point of view. I tried to give myself. And when I gave myself I also gave my emotions. Soon I found my emotions running along in a most satisfactory way!

The truth is that you cannot in the beginning say, "I'm going to make my heart go pitter-patter when I'm in the presence of this person." You can't do it. You start off on another basis and you let the pitter-patter come later.

Third—Christian love accepts another person where he or she is. We usually start with another person where *we* are. And so in our little Christian chats with a person—in our conferencing, in our classes, in our preaching—we preach what we need to preach rather than what the other person needs to hear. Or we teach the children what the children do not need to hear, but what the teacher needs to say. We minister to ourselves rather than to others.

While love will produce a new quality of life, it does not demand this new quality of life as a precondition. (1) We, although unacceptable, have been accepted by God; therefore, (2) we must accept the unacceptable and not ask that they be acceptable before we accept them.

Herein is God's love revealed to us: while we were yet sinners, Christ died for us. So Christ broke through the circle of our deep need, and he said, "I will so love you that in my love you will come to be what you ought to be." But he did not say, "You work on it pretty hard and then one day when you get good enough I will come down and love you a little bit." The point is, love is always building bridges, and it throws a bridge over to the place where the other person is.

Now there are several dangers. One is that we will throw this bridge *down* to the poor duffer in need. Here we are the righteous ones, we are the adequate ones, and we are throwing our bridge across. We are throwing out a lifeline. We are going to pull him in.

Whenever you and I throw a bridge across to somebody in need, we who are helpless are throwing it across to another who is helpless. We who are sinners are throwing it across to another sinner. *All* of us are in need. It just so happens that we have met One who is very strong and very adequate and who means life itself. He wants both of us to be able to move back and forth across this bridge in his presence. Then we get away from this self-righteousness. Whenever we help another we help ourselves perhaps more than we help the other person.

There is, however, another problem. Sometimes, rather than reaching down, we remove a person from us by putting her up on a pedestal. And so we have an idol on our hands. Here is a person who is perfect. Here is a person who will never let us down. Here is a person who embodies our spiritual hopes and dreams—who becomes a trustee for our own spiritual concerns. As long as I know this person and can watch her sitting up on this pedestal, I don't have to do anything other than worship the Father. But this makes the person on the pedestal very lonely. I have no right to do that to another. Furthermore, this makes me very lonely. And, because all of us have feet of clay, one day the idol will come tumbling down from the pedestal.

We accept others where they are in the knowledge that, when this is a genuine acceptance—not one which tries to rub out the real problems of the picture—we are not calling white black, or black white. We do not say this person has no faults. All of us have faults. We are strange mixtures, are we not? Of weakness and strength; of good and evil. All of us are creatures of faith and lack of faith. To accept others is to see them as this strange mixture, not to write off all that is bad and thus have our vision be cloudy. If we can accept others where they are, God will bring them to the place where they ought to be.

Fourth—Christian love sets no limits to its love. Ordinary human love is always a conditional self-giving. It says, "You can come in only so close to me, and there you must stop." You've seen this, haven't you? A person can put up psychological defenses, and you can feel it just as much as though a sign had been put up saying, "Don't touch. It's all right for you to come this close, but don't get past this point. Let's don't hit any pay dirt. Let's keep it shallow." This is true of most of us. We have our little fences which guard us. Also, we have our limits as to how far we will go in giving ourselves to another. We have the feeling that, having given so much time and so much money and so much energy and effort, more could scarcely be required of any human being.

Christian love throws away all limits saying. "I may have a difficult time doing it, but come on in just as far as you can come. I want you; I need you. Please come. It may take a little time for me to learn to do it, but I will love you with a concern which has no limits. I will simply balance the needs of this person and this person and this person, and as God leads me and enables me to do it, I will be available to you in any way possible. I belong to you!"

One is willing to change one's own way of life, is willing to give up one's own legitimate satisfactions in the interests of a sister or brother. We no longer try to play around with the minimal standards, asking, "Is it all right for a Christian to do this?" We ask, "What can I do to be most helpful to my brother? What will most strengthen my sister? If what I am doing—which is perfectly legitimate—is damaging another's life, I will give it up even though it is perfectly harmless in itself."

Paul said that we who are strong ought to bear with the failings of the weak. Remember the illustration he used about whether it was right to eat meat which had been offered to idols? This was his argument: "It is all right for me to eat this food which has been offered to the idol because I know that there is no reality in the idol. The food is perfectly good. It has simply sat there on the table for a little while. Why throw it away?" But suppose there comes into this pagan temple a brother who does not know that there is no reality in that idol. For him to eat this food would be wrong. Then suppose he sees me eating the meat and is influenced by me. I will have hurt the brother for whom Christ died. As long as I live I will eat no meat if it hurts my brother.

There are no limits to what a Christian will do in order to lift, to prop up, and to help a sister or brother who is stamped with the image of God. This means having an unlimited willingness to work for others. If it involves money, and the money will really help the other, then the money will be available. If it is a matter of time, the time is available. Nothing will be unavailable, for self-giving is unlimited.

This love that sets no limits involves the willingness to give life physically if need be. Stephen gave his, James his, Peter his, Paul his. In our present day, Dietrich Bonhoeffer gave his life. And down through two thousand years of Christian history there have been many, many martyrs who have given their lives for others. Jesus himself said, "Greater love has no man than this, that a man lay down his life for his friends" (John 15:13, *RSV*)—the symbol of total, utter self-giving.

You say, "If I could ever learn to do this, wouldn't it be wonderful?" It is wonderful in a way, but, interestingly enough, love like this always meets resistance on the part of the person loved. Partly because we love so awkwardly we threaten the very self-consistency of those we love, for they find they have to be real, they have to face areas in their own lives which they do not want to face. They are in the presence of reality at last. And so we meet resistance. Sometimes this resistance boils to the point where it wants to put us to death. That is what happened in the case of Christ. They put him on a cross.

We have many subtle ways of putting our contemporaries on a cross, and of being put on a cross ourselves. "Blessed are those who are persecuted for righteousness' sake, for theirs is the kingdom of heaven. Blessed are you when men revile you and persecute you, and utter all kinds of evil against you falsely on my account" (Matt. 5:10–12, *RSV*). What do you do? Here we come to the point of unlimited forgiveness. You forgive the person who resists. You forgive the person who returns this love awkwardly.

When Peter began to get hold of this truth, it was so difficult for him that he said, "Christ, I would like to get this thing straightened out. I'm beginning to see it. But how many times do I have to do this?" And then he made a little proposed estimate. He said, "Should I do it seven times?" I'm sure he thought that was a very generous figure. Anybody who could do this seven times is pretty wonderful. And Jesus said, "Peter, you didn't catch it at all, did you? I say to you not seven times, but seventy times seven!" (Matt. 18:21–22, paraphrased). This figure of speech simply meant, "Keep it up indefinitely." Forgiveness is to be unlimited.

What is your reaction to all this? I hope you say, "This is impossible. You just don't know the sort of man I'm married to." Or, "If you knew the sort of woman I have to live with, you would know this is just impossible." Or, "If you knew all those little undercurrents that are played out in the office! Forgiveness may be possible within the bounds of a Christian community, but in an office—a government office?! You just don't know."

Of course, the fact is that this sort of love *is* impossible. You just can't do it. If you throw up your hands in despair and say, " I am commanded to do this but I simply cannot do it"—that's wonderful! That's exactly where God wants you. God knows you cannot love in this way on demand.

This kind of love comes as a supernatural grace. Having looked at the cross, having your heart broken wide open, you come to know that God's grace is surrounding you and you rest back in it. You know you have been loved with this sort of love. And simply because you have entered into this love, you are able to splash it around so that it touches anybody who comes close to you. For this is a supernatural grace and there are people who love in this way. I have seen them. I know them, and you recognize in them just enough of Jesus to make you uncomfortable.

"Love one another as I have loved you." This is what it means to be a Christian. And if we do not love this way, we are not yet Christian!

8

Forgiveness—A Start

∾

In 1959 The Church of the Saviour was excited about the dream of a Christian coffee house to be named the Potter's House. In the midst of this excitement, the need for forgiveness was recognized as being just as great as ever.

Do you remember the Jubilee year among the Jews—the time when debts were forgiven? Everyone was free and able to start over again, clean and fresh. Perhaps the gift which would make us all happiest would be the ability to forgive one another, to release whatever we hold against another—and to extend forgiveness to every person who has ever hurt us.

Jesus talked about the great need of people to forgive others. He made it very plain that when we are unable or unwilling to do this, we cut ourselves off from the very life of God. There is no way to receive God's grace unless we are able to forgive those who have hurt us.

I find that most good people (and most of us are good people in this sense) feel they have nothing very much to forgive. Good people find it hard to think of anything that needs forgiving. What a noble thought! But I doubt that it is true. I have an idea that every one of us has a great deal to forgive. Some of us might find ourselves shocked to discover how much we do have to forgive.

In all probability there are many people in our lives who have not been forgiven, and there are many offenses against us which have not been forgiven! Life is full of hurt. It is virtually impossible to grow to maturity without having had serious hurt inflicted upon us along the way. We can look at those injuries in a lot of different ways.

Somewhere in the past, usually in the early years of childhood, the hurt comes when the essential self is damaged. When I become aware

69

of what has taken place in the lives of most people that I know, I wonder how so many stupid, foolish, unbelievable things could have been done—things which were just wrong, things which hurt, things which mar the very image of Christ which is the essential self.

Not only are there those things which were done to us, but there are those things which were not done—things that have driven us into a sort of isolation. We have protected ourselves by adopting facades, by not being ourselves, and those free, spontaneous, open persons we were and were intended to be have been distorted and damaged.

One of the most painful things which can happen to us is to doubt whether anyone has ever cared to know what was going on in our inner life. While talking to a friend a few days ago I asked, "Do you have the feeling that anyone has ever really wanted to know what was going on in your inner life?"

She said, "No."

"Not your mother?"

"No, not my mother."

"Not anybody?"

She said, "No, not anybody. Once in a while I have had the feeling that somebody wanted to know what was going on in me because she needed to know for her own sake, not for mine." How amazing it is that a person can come to maturity and honestly have the feeling that no one has ever wanted to know what was going on in that real inner self. Admitting that this is one of the most serious injuries ever inflicted on a person, you and I are doing that very thing every day to someone. If we ourselves have been the victims of this kind of neglect, we are probably having a very difficult time sensing that we are people of worth. We are suffering probably more than we can ever let anyone know from depression, anxiety, and frustration.

Let us consider not only past hurts but also about what is happening to us in the present. Things have gone wrong with us this past week. The structures of our life don't suit us. We feel that we are not loved, we are not heard, and people do not care. We feel this in our home situation, and often in our work situation.

∾ *Dealing with Injuries* ∾

Life is full of hurts, and we have much to forgive. How do we deal with injuries? Several ways, some better than others.

The first reaction may be one of vengeance. You say, "I don't desire vengeance on anyone." However, the forms of vengeance we practice are sometimes subtle. Vengeance says, "I'll get even." We are resentful toward those who are unkind to us. When our feelings are hurt, we may respond by a sort of icy silence.

A still more subtle way of being vengeful is to hurt oneself, to become ill, to begin to fail, to develop a will to failure. Paul Tillich terms this tendency "hidden suicide." We destroy ourselves inch by inch. In this way we say to those who have hurt us, "I'll let you know really how much pain I have borne. I'll let you know how rough it has been. I want you to know how it hurts." The trouble is that this way of dealing with the pain is not mutual, not something which we do with another person but something we do alone.

The second way in which we deal with hurts is to say, in effect, "Well, it really didn't hurt. I'll put the whole thing out of my mind. I'll go on as if it never happened." Then the injury keeps functioning as a source of hidden infection. Covered with a bandage, the wound does not heal. The fact is that it did hurt. Any doctor can tell you that the body cries out, "It did hurt!" The mind cries out, "It did hurt!" The emotions cry out, "It did hurt!" We can go around denying our pain, but a part of us knows that it *did* hurt.

In the third way of dealing with these hurts we simply say: "Well, I am who I am." We build dreams of superiority and say, "Some day they'll realize who I am." Or, "I don't care about this thing for myself, but it is a matter of principle." Haven't you heard that time and time again?

The fourth way in which most good people deal with hurt is the highest moral response we can make. It is to say, "This thing is really all right. I forgive you. It would hurt me and it would hurt you if I didn't forgive you." Or, "It would be unhealthy for me to hold grudges, for me to nurse this hurt. It's beneath me to do it. Surely I will extend forgiveness. I will be magnanimous. I will forgive you." I have an idea that this is the way you and I usually deal with an injury; but this is a moral response, the highest moral response that a person can make. However, a moral response is not real forgiveness.

⁓ *Christian Forgiveness* ⁓

Christian forgiveness offers a new openness toward the person or the situation that has caused the hurt, finding a way through the other's resistance and endeavoring to learn what caused him or her to inflict the hurt in the first place.

The tragic thing is that often we do just the opposite of that which is needed. When some brittle or unbending person is curt to us or makes a little remark probably not meant to offend, we become sullen and withdrawn. We begin to nurse our injury by telling some friend about it. By the time we have told half a dozen friends in confidence—always in confidence, because we wouldn't want to hurt anybody!—the one who wounded us has become isolated.

What does that isolated person need? She needs us to move out toward her and embrace her. She was curt and brittle to us because of a hurt she had on the inside. We know that. In spite of our own hurt, we need to reach out and embrace her—rather than running around talking to other people creating a pocket of isolation for her. This is exactly the opposite of what she needs. Forgiveness means continuing to try to find a way through to the other person. It means giving to another that which is most priceless to us, even if it is trampled under-foot, even if we are destroyed in the process.

Forgiveness keeps saying, "I will find a way through. The defensive armor of this person is very thick and, although I don't see the way now to penetrate it, there must be a way. If it takes the rest of my life and eternity, I will discover a way. I will get through to this person." When we have really extended forgiveness to another person, there is a new openness. Just as God keeps saying, "I will find a way through to my child," we say to the one who has hurt us (or we say in our spirit), "I will find a way. I will find a way through."

Things to Remember ~
~ When Making an Effort to Forgive

The ability to forgive is a grace granted by God. We cannot really do this thing unless God enables us to do it. I do not believe that we can forgive another person through our own efforts. When we endeavor to forgive on our own, we make the highest moral response, but this is not forgiveness in the Christian sense.

We ourselves stand desperately in need of forgiveness. We are aware of what has been done to us, but it is difficult for us to see the many ways in which we isolate and hurt other people. Indeed, we may have inflicted much more hurt on other people than has been received by us.

We have been the occasion of their loneliness, and we have been the occasion of their fears. We have defaulted at crucial moments. The stupidity of what we have done and have not done is unbelievable.

How have we dealt with our own sins against others? With remorse, with good resolutions—going through the cycle of remorse and good resolutions until finally we become so discouraged we fall into indifference. We are helped to extend forgiveness when we realize that the only sure way open to us is to cry to God, "God, be merciful to me, a sinner."

For instance, suppose that God has something for us to do, such as bringing a healing clinic into existence. Suppose we delay; suppose we do not catch the dream. Suppose it never really comes into existence in the way God intended. Then you and I are responsible for denying opportunity to all those persons who might have discovered life there, who failed to be visited by the grace of God as they might have been. We are responsible because we failed to enter into that dream of God. Every mission God gives us is vitally important. In these failures of ours we are just as responsible as we think our parents are for what they did not give us. There are so many ways in which we have been remiss!

Another important thing: Whenever we think about extending forgiveness, we must remember that it is a sinner—not a righteous person—who extends forgiveness to a fellow sinner. We are not on a pedestal reaching down to forgive some poor soul who has hurt us. We are not extending forgiveness from some position of superiority. First of all, we must cry out to God, "God, forgive me." Then perhaps we are ready to extend forgiveness to another.

Before we try to forgive the one who has inflicted the hurt, take the hurt and look at it. Taste it and drink it. This sounds un-Christian. Time and time again when I have talked to people about this, they say, "This doesn't ring true to me. This is un-Christian. Why stir things up? Why rehash and evoke feelings of hatred and hostility and resentment?"

The reason is that we simply cannot turn over a hurt to God until we have been willing to face it. As long as we are running away from how much it hurt, I doubt that we will be able to give it to God. The thing to do is to pull it out, look at it, and discover that this thing has brought more pain than we can say—causing failure in certain areas, causing problems at the point of marriage, causing difficulties here, and here, and there. We taste the hurt. We drink it right down to the dregs. Then, having looked at it, not avoiding or trying to repress it, we can consciously take the hurt to God, who can bring to us healing and renewal.

What helps most in my effort to forgive is to look at the cost to God of my redemption, of my forgiveness, and of everyone else's forgiveness—to look at the cross. Finally, the only thing that ever really melts our hearts and enables us to be new and different, the only thing that ever really enables us to extend forgiveness to another, is seeing what it has cost God.

Every once in a while I am able to bear the pain and the hurt of another person and, to be honest, it hurts. If I, in my human way, can carry the need of another person and it hurts this much, what must it do to God, who drinks in the hurt of all of humanity, of every person who is lonely, every person who knows estrangement, and every person who carries a heavy burden? How can the heart of God bear it without breaking? But, of course, it did break the heart of God. This is the meaning of Calvary.

I have a favorite fairy tale about a young student who loved a lady very much. She told him that he could take her to the ball if he would bring her a red, red rose that would match her gown. He went out into the garden to find the rose, but there were only white roses—not even one red rose. The student lay down in the dust and wept.

A nightingale flew by and asked the student what was wrong. He told the nightingale, "I cannot take my love to the ball unless I have a red, red rose, and there are no red roses in the garden. I've gone to the different bushes, and they have simply laughed at me. There is no red rose."

The nightingale went to the garden and began to talk to the bushes. One bush which had a white rose in its bosom said, "No, there are no red roses. But there is one way for you to have a red rose, and that is for you to press your bosom against the thorn, sing your sweetest song, and let your very life's blood flow into the vine. Then the white rose will become a red, red rose."

So the nightingale pressed its breast against the thorn and began to sing its sweetest song. As the blood of the nightingale poured out, as it sang its most beautiful song, the white rose began to be tinted with pink. Finally the petals turned a deep red. But as the rose became a red, red rose, the voice of the nightingale became weaker, and in just a few moments the nightingale lay dead.

In the morning the student went to the garden and found the rose. He cried out in joy because he had a rose to carry to his love. He plucked it and went to her saying, "Here is the red, red rose. You said I might take you to the ball."

But she turned and said, "Did you not know that the chamberlain's son sent me jewels? Everyone knows that jewels are more costly than flowers. Anyway, I have decided to wear another gown and the jewels match my gown." So she flung the red rose into the road and a passing coach crushed it.

The student went back to his room saying, "I think I will take up philosophy, because philosophy is safer than love." He closed his door and went back to his books.[1]

Jesus told a story: The owner of a vineyard sent one of his servants and they beat him. He sent another and they stoned him. He sent still another and they killed him. Finally, he said, "What can I do? How can I get through to them?" So he said, "I'll send my son—they will receive him." But they killed the Son.

In this story Jesus was telling just what God did and what forgiveness means to God. In this same way God breaks through to you and me.

Every now and then I get a glimpse of God's merciful forgiveness, and when I do, there is no way I can hold in my heart any resentment, hostility, or hatred toward anyone in all the world.

Note

[1] Oscar Wilde, "The Nightingale and the Rose," in *The Fisherman and His Soul and Other Fairy Tales* (New York: Farrar & Rinehart, 1929), pp. 131-42.

9

Forgiveness—A Continuing Experience

~

In the decade after the founding of The Church of the Saviour, Gordon continued to stress the crucial importance of forgiveness.

We are all weary of hearing about anxiety, and we wish we could be done with it. But we are destined to live with it. We all experience primal anxiety, and we shall know it all our days. It is the price of our freedom, but it tempts us to misuse our freedom. This basic condition is aggravated, in turn, by neurotic anxiety brought on by malignant, wrong relationships with others, whether during childhood or in the present moment.

Our natural reaction when we feel anxious is to try to secure ourselves, to try to make ourselves safe. The root meaning of the word *salvation* is "safety." So, rather than accepting the Savior who, in Christian thinking, is the Lord Jesus Christ, we try to become our own saviors. The harder the problem, the harder we try. Christianity says that when we depend on our own strength and power, our situation is hopeless, because the more we try, the worse the problem becomes. We simply succeed in cutting ourselves off from God, the very ground of our being, and the more anxious and driven we become.

The only answer is to let God come to us where we are in our present helpless predicament—to accept God's acceptance—and thereby to accept ourselves, and to accept one another, to accept life and its vicissitudes, and let the rebellion be over. When reconciliation takes place, we have laid down the arms of our resistance, we have surrendered the throne. The rigid, tight, threatened self has become a relaxed, humbled, chastened self. Chastened, because at last we can see how foolish we have been, what a ridiculous figure we have been cutting. We see something of the terrible cost of it all to God Almighty, because there stands the eternal cross, which no one can tear down. We come to see something of the unspeakable cost of our rebellion (our sin) in the lives of other people. We know we cannot go back and do much about it. Only God can go back.

In our rebellion we have tried to kill God himself. We did not like the structure of life; we rebelled against it; we tried to set up our own structure, and this is to try to kill God. This is how mad we have been, how insane, how sick.

And what has God done? God, continuing to love us through it all, has simply taken all our actions to heart, seeking to interpret and make clear to us our sickness and weakness so we could understand. Moreover, only God can heal the hurts we have caused others by our rebellious lashings at them or by our superior self-containment. Rebellion against God takes many different forms.

To see the situation fully, we must unconditionally surrender to God. To ask for a conditional surrender is not to see the situation at all; it is to get hints that there is a problem somewhere, to suspect our sin and need, but it is not to see it clearly. To have this thing dawn clearly for us is to realize that we have not one little strip of sovereign territory left.

This forgiveness, this reconciliation, this justification—call it what you will—comes about because God has hung out the sheets of heaven, letting us know that we can come home, even if we come from a far country, and even if we are limping when we come. God is ready to grant forgiveness. Our part is to be willing to look squarely at ourselves, to search our own hearts, to be led to repentance, and then to confession.

This experience is so earth-shaking that we are forever bound to the one who delivers us. God brings us into a togetherness with others who have also been delivered into a community of the delivered. The Christian fellowship, the Christian Church, has mediated this experience to us in the first place. This is the way we came into it. Perhaps we heard the faithful proclamation of the Gospel by a minister. Or it may be that a faithful layperson, a colleague at work, said something that led us into the presence of Christ. While we were reading the Scriptures one day the good news dawned for us. We may have been listening to a great piece of music. The Scriptures were preserved for us by the church and the great music was the music of the church. This experience came to us, somehow, because of the church.

No other experience in the world is like this one. We were dead in our trespasses and sins, and now we are alive together in Christ. We were no people, and now we are God's people. We are under God's destiny. We have encountered something unique.

Sometimes we ask, "What is really unique about this church to which I belong?" The point is that every work of God is unique. If God has brought this church into existence, then it is unique; it is wonderful; it is something to become excited about. We are not raving about ourselves at all. We are not even raving about our friends whom we love. We are raving because God still acts in human life! Not to recognize this action is effectively to cut ourselves off from any action of God in life.

The experience which we call reconciliation, justification, or forgiveness is, in a sense, complete. It is complete in that we can say, "This has really happened to me." This is not an external theological fiction, but something within our spirit that is able to cry out, "Abba, Father," in response to the Holy Spirit, which has spoken to our spirit. We have had an experience of meeting with God.

The center of life has been shifted from self to God. No longer are we trying to make ourselves secure. We have placed our security into God's hands. God makes us safe. God makes us free, and at last our own frantic efforts can cease.

In another sense this experience is incomplete, because all the rest of our days we will be finding our peace and our meaning in this God who continues the same yesterday, today, and forever. From this God we must draw our life in every moment. From this God, in humble dependence and by grace, we must draw continuing forgiveness, for we shall continue to fail to respond as God would have us do. And we shall continue to misuse our freedom. We shall do it today, and we shall do it in the future.

Let us look for a moment at the paradox of our faith. Christianity says that a new age has dawned. Something broke into human life when Christ came. Something unprecedented happened in his resurrection. Life is not the same, because a new springtime has come to our planet. The paradox arises out of the fact that this new age has not yet been consummated. In a sense we are in an interim period between the breaking open of the powers of the new age and the consummation of the new age.

What will this consummation be? We can say only that it will be a perfect condition for redeemed souls. What more need anyone say?

The powers of the new age have already dawned. The age will be consummated. This is the hope of glory.

We face another paradox. Here I am, a new creation in this new age, and you, if you are in Christ, are also a new creation. The problem is that the old self is not yet completely dead! Our freedom continues to tempt us, and we continue to sin. We do not sin quite as we did before, but nevertheless we continue to sin. So here we are, ambivalent creatures. We must have continuing forgiveness. We must continue to depend upon God every moment.

Actually, I am in danger every moment because I can misuse my new freedom, a greater freedom than I had before. Every time I properly use my freedom, I am given more freedom. The dimension is expanded. My freedom is enhanced. But the greater the freedom, the more serious it is to misuse it. Thus, enhanced freedom becomes another source of anxiety. With this in mind Kierkegaard speaks of walking on the razor's edge. And Paul wrote, "I buffet my own body lest when I preach to others, I myself become a castaway." Here is Paul, one of the great Christian spirits of all time, saying, "I'd better watch out, because it may be that I can preach to others, but in the very process of the preaching I may become a castaway" (1 Cor. 9:27, paraphrased).

We often hear people say that coming into the Christian life is the way to be saved from our anxiety. We are so eager to be saved that we feel, "I'd better hurry up and get this behind me quickly because I want to be saved." This insecurity, this anxiety drives us so that we simulate the valid experience instead of having a genuine one.

Even a simulated experience is rather humiliating. Our reaction may be, "Thank goodness that experience is behind me. Surrendering to Christ was terrible while it lasted. It destroyed my dignity. But I had to go through it, since it is said that this is the gateway to the Christian life. Now, with salvation behind me, I can get back to normal. I can get on with life." The fact is that this experience, when genuine, can never be behind us. This life, and the grace of God it offers, is the only life there is. So to "get on with life" apart from this is to get on with death—eternal death. We do not look back and say, "Wasn't that a terrible thing?" We look back and say, "That was the most priceless experience I could ever have. God is all in all, and I can lose myself in God. Isn't it wonderful that I can continue to give myself to God through all the years? This same God will come back to me in just this same way when I do not deserve it, and I can give myself back in full, free surrender. What a God I have!"

The experience of knowing continuing forgiveness implies acknowledgment of, and attention to, certain accompanying factors. Our emotions are easily stirred and, as the weeks go by, life may settle back on the old level and we won't know that same new freedom and joy.

To prevent this retrogression perhaps in every life there should be at least a daily self-searching. We are as honest as we know how to be with ourselves; we look squarely at ourselves, and then we let this self-searching move on to repentance, and to confession.

We are not to be morbid, but we should be specific. Instead of just saying that we have difficulty with the problem of loving, we might say something like this: "When I'm honest, I know I don't really love these people. They irritate me; they upset me. The only reason I hang around is that I don't know where else to go. But if I don't care for these people, then I do not really care for God, for God yearns over them and loves them."

Take a look at this ugly little spirit that we carry around in our hearts. We call it by so many names; everything is wrong with so many others, so many situations. But we ought to say, "God, the trouble is that I am in rebellion against you. I'm in rebellion against my life. I don't like the way you and life and all its vicissitudes have worked things out for me at this present moment." If we could say those things to God in all honesty, it would save us a lot of time, and it would save a lot of heartache on the part of other people.

But let me warn you. Self-searching can go on and on, past the point where we know very well what to do about it! There is a point when one should stop self-searching and do something more painful: repent. Somehow we just won't do it. We won't look at ourselves with that additional light which we almost have (and could have if we would). We will not humble ourselves and simply say, "God, here I am. Take me. I'm yours." Such a sincere declaration would involve us in a closer relationship with and a deeper indebtedness to God. It is easier to keep on with the self-analysis. Therefore, we must discover the limits and move on.

The second thing that Christians have found to be important in ongoing forgiveness is frequent worship with participation in the sacraments. A primary need in our times together is to hear God's word of absolution. As a people, we have been so far from what we know even in our own sinful hearts we could be—what God would have us be.

The question is, who will forgive us? Who will pronounce us clean? Who will grant us the gift of being able to overcome our areas of failure, our insensitivity, and our dullness? We experience only a little trickle of life, when we should be overflowing with the promised rivers of living water. Who will forgive us? God will—our God against whom we have most deeply sinned.

At the conclusion of a time of worship when we have faced real issues such as these, we may feel battered and heavy. We feel heavy when we leave because we are resisting and fighting the forgiveness offered by God. We can hardly get out; we can scarcely drag ourselves away. Better to leave in the glad awareness that we are right with God—that we have been pronounced clean—because from penitent hearts we have made confession and have accepted God's promise of forgiveness. If only we could tiptoe out in awed adoration, bursting to tell the news of the God whom we have met. God is the real issue, not whether we agree with this concept or that.

Christians say the central act of worship is the Eucharist or communion, the Lord's Supper. In this service we take the symbol of broken bread, which represents the broken body of Christ. We take the wine, which represents the shed blood of Christ. We say we are offering ourselves to God through these concrete symbols. Some people have difficulty with the communion service. They do not want to deal with sacred symbols such as these because they are not really ready to offer themselves. They say they simply do not understand. Through the Lord's Supper we symbolize our self-offering to God. And the very symbol that we use for this offering is the channel of grace through which God comes to us. To try to give anything to God is embarrassing, because God uses exactly the same channel to return so much to us that we cannot contain it.

The same is true of all the sacrifices we make—the sacrifice of prayer, the sacrifice of living with the Scriptures, the sacrifice of money. Whatever it is, as we give ourselves through these offerings, which represent ourselves, they become channels of grace through which God comes back to us.

If we are having trouble at the point of these sacrifices, these symbols of our offerings, we are probably not ready at the deeper places of our being to offer ourselves.

Within the context of a holy fellowship I am able to look at myself and repent and give myself to God. This illumines the statement, "Outside the church there is no salvation." A holy fellowship is the community of those who have had this experience, of those who are redeemed, of those who are accepted. Therefore, they know a little something about accepting other people. They help us believe that God continues to do the thing which seems incredible to us. If we can live within the fabric of an accepting community, we are able to believe that somehow God keeps pouring out God's life in just this way.

What do we mean by an accepting community? Let me tell you what it means on an elementary level. One day I was sitting in a group listening to a conversation. One of the persons said, "This is what happened to me when I was with a gang down in Florida," and he went on talking about what took place under those circumstances. The other man said, "That reminds me of what happened when I was in an opium den in Haifa." And they went on talking. I looked around to see whether there were any lifted eyebrows or widened eyes as a result of this conversation, and no one had been in the least disconcerted by it.

Acceptance on this level, however, is not as easy as sometimes we assume it to be, either for the person or for the community. We should never take sin casually, for this is not the way to love a person. Sin, which separates us from God, is never to be taken lightly. At the same time we recognize that this is the common attitude of most people, and we have discovered the sinfulness of our own being.

We are not unduly surprised when another discloses personal sinfulness. Not that we don't take it seriously, but because we know something of the depths of sin within our own lives. We are dealing with something we know. At this point, however, the church may not know how to help the sinner feel the comfort of God's people. We must never minimize the terrible isolation that a person feels because of sin.

In many ways it is much easier to help the gross sinner feel the consolation of God's people than it is to accept a person in the later stages of development. We often find it more difficult to accept someone who has ceased to be a raw, obvious sinner, because at the earlier stage that person usually represented no threat to us.

Because some of us may still have a notion that the far country is rather enticing, we may experience a kind of threat. Learning the particulars of someone's straying into sinfulness we find it difficult to accept that person because, if the truth be known, we are envious. We find ourselves wondering whether Christian people, the moralists and all the rest, have not tried to cut us out of a little fun which might be ours if we could sneak into the far country for a little while. We wish we could go for just a short visit.

If you feel that urge, maybe you should try it out. But it is a sad journey with very little glamour about it. Ask somebody who has been there. Go with that person beneath the superficial surface of life and learn what it was like.

Usually, though, there is not too much threat at that level. The problem comes when a person begins to develop a certain uniqueness, an attractive individuality, seems different from any person you have ever known before, and emerges as different from yourself! Here acceptance may prove difficult.

When you categorize a person—and this is a form of judging—you deepen the isolation and increase the anxiety of that person. Categories are not good anyway, because the Christian's life is moving and does not fit into any one category for any length of time.

Now to "tolerate" anyone because of his or her difference is to increase that person's sense of isolation. But if you can be grateful for this difference— if once in a while you can express your gratitude—that will reduce the anxiety. This does not exclude honesty. In fact, it requires honesty.

A spurious form of honesty is honesty without courage. We can be terribly honest and bold expressing ourselves about our brothers and sisters. We will be commended for it because we are "not afraid to speak." This can even be a prestige-gaining mechanism within the fellowship. Others, accused of not being honest, are free enough to speak but, realizing that they have spent too much of their lives speaking in just this way, would rather have their tongues cut out than do anything to hurt the delicate fabric which the Holy Spirit holds together. There is such a thing as being free enough to speak honestly about a brother or sister, but there is a point beyond which one is free enough not to speak—not even to think in an accusing way—for then one becomes an accuser of another. One of the few rules we get straight from Jesus' lips is given in Matthew:

> "If your brother sins against you, go and tell him his fault,
> between you and him alone. If he listens to you, you have
> gained your brother. But if he does not listen, take one or two

others along with you, that every word may be confirmed by the
evidence of two or three witnesses. If he refuses to listen to
them, tell it to the church; and if he refuses to listen even to the
church, let him be to you as a Gentile and a tax collector."
(Matt. 18:15, *RSV*)

Not only should we be honest to the person about whom we are
concerned, but we should be honest to that person at the proper time.
And not only is there a time to be honest about another's incapacities,
problems, and difficulties; there is also a time to be honest about the
fine, wonderful qualities of that person's life. We must remember that it
is much easier to be honest about the few things about another that
threaten us and that we don't like, than to be honest about the scores
of ways in which the grace of God shines through. We ourselves have
many things to resolve. My unconscious may be a veritable cesspool of
writhing, devastating emotions which in others may be less severe.
Feeling a bit envious of a person who is not having to undergo my
same misery, I suspect that that person is just not being honest! Her
smiling exterior must be covering up some weakness that she ought to
be facing. She should be more honest, like me!

Some people never have to go through what others go through. On
the other hand, some have already gone through a torturous hell and
have come to the place where their lives reflect the heavenly light and
a divine gentleness and sweetness. The Scripture promises that when
we are in Christ, out of our inner lives shall flow rivers of living water.
We have known those of whom this is true.

As the months and the years go by, we shall learn increasingly to
make the Christian community a truly accepting community.

The experience of reconciliation will be continued each day as we
find time for a period of self-searching leading to repentance, to a
voluntary surrender of ourselves to God and to the appropriation of
forgiveness in our own lives. When this becomes a daily cleansing
experience, we shall know our sinful and neurotic anxiety to be forgiven, and we shall have the faith to live through the primal anxiety
which is the lot of each one of us.

A necessary part of this continuing process is corporate worship
with God's people, along with the celebration of the sacrament of
communion. Every service of worship should be a time when we offer
ourselves to God in voluntary self-surrender and, in that offering of

ourselves and in the sacrament of communion, we receive from God in a mysterious way the gift of peace and life. Charles Stinnette says:

> The bread and wine of the communion service represent sacred offerings whereby we symbolize the offering of our own lives to God. They are means of expressing thanksgiving to God, and the vehicle of his assurance of acceptance and grace. They symbolize living as an integral part of an accepted and accepting community, a reconciled community, and, consequently, one which is always offering reconciliation. In one's time of daily prayer and in times of corporate worship, these are the ways in which we receive the continuing acceptance and grace of God, until life comes to be a paean of spontaneous praise.[1]

Our community can never be perfect. Don't expect it to be perfect. Perfection will come when the interim period, which we call life, is over and the hope of glory has been consummated. But isn't it amazing that anyone can love us just as we are? What do they get out of it? The only thing I can figure out is that the Holy Spirit is really with us. Somehow our people do love in an amazing way. And this enables me to enter continually into the forgiveness of God, by which I live.

Note

[1] Charles Stinnette, Jr., "Toward Resolving Anxiety in Christian Community," in *Anxiety and Faith: Resolving Anxiety in Christian Community* (Greenwich, Conn.: The Seabury Press, 1955), pp. 167-68.

10

Intercessory Prayer

~

In February 1956 The Church of the Saviour was not quite ten years old. In this first decade Gordon focused on the basics of the Christian life, including prayer.

Almost every Christian knows in a vague way that we are expected to pray for other people. We know that this is called intercession or intercessory prayer. We also know that we, ourselves, do not pray very much for other people. Certainly it is not the primary mission of our lives. Usually we have what we feel are fairly substantial objections to the whole procedure. They run something like this:

What sort of God would withhold good things—things God would like to give—from people because there was not someone around at the proper time to ask? Does a God of love have to be cajoled for attention? What about the poor people who have no one to pray for them? Does God desert them because there is nobody handy to pray?

Here is a person that God wants to make well. Is God impotent to make that person well until someone reminds God of the need?

A young man struggles with a temptation which rages like a fire within him. Is there no cessation from this struggle, no strength until some fellow human being tells God that help is necessary?

A young mother becomes entirely exhausted. Is there no relief from God until someone prays for her?

All these questions and others we ask have to do with queries about the validity of prayer. They are important questions, which we have every right to ask. And there are answers to them. But I would suggest that these questions are not as profound as we believe them to be. The real reasons we do not pray may lie deeper within ourselves:

Perhaps we do not pray because we do not love enough—we do not care deeply. Perhaps we cannot get outside ourselves long enough to intercede for another, or we do not really care whether God's purpose is being fulfilled in the life of another person.

We want our sleep more than we feel the need to pray for another.

Our food is more important than intercessory prayer.

It is devastating to think that we may have been given the privilege and responsibility of affecting another person forever, eternally. That responsibility so frightens us that immediately we say, "Well, surely God is not the sort of God who would withhold benefits from someone because I do not pray." We do not want to feel that ours might be a decisive role in the life of another. Surely God would not allow that.

Now I do not care to argue for the reasonableness of intercessory prayer, although there is a place for that. I will simply say that for the Christian who is devoted to the Master, it is enough to know that Jesus prayed for others. Jesus prayed for children. They brought babies for him to touch. Jesus prayed for the sick. When he was ready to heal the blind man, he lifted up his eyes to heaven and prayed. He prayed for his disciples. He said to Simon, "Simon . . . Satan demanded to have you, that he might sift you like wheat, but I have prayed for you that your faith may not fail" (Luke 22:31–32, *RSV*). Jesus prayed for his enemies. "Father, forgive them; for they know not what they do" (Luke 23:34, *RSV*). He prayed that God would send forth laborers into his harvest, for he obeyed his own injunction, "Pray therefore the Lord of the harvest to send out laborers into his harvest" (Matt. 9:38, *RSV*). He prayed for his followers down to the end of time who would belong to the community of faith. He said, "I do not pray for these only, but also for those who are to believe in me through their word" (John 17:20, *RSV*). This is one thing that we know about the life of Jesus—his was a life filled with intercessory prayer.

The same thing is true in the life of Paul, the chief exponent of the Christian faith in the early days of the movement. Turn to Thessalonians, turn to Corinthians, to Romans, to Philippians, to any one of the epistles, and you will find his great heart reaching out and undergirding the people that he loved.

Perhaps this whole matter of intercessory prayer is simpler than we believe it to be. First, in order really to pray for another person, we must have the right concept of God and we must trust God.

The Christian God is not indifferent—never apathetic. Our God is always eager to give gifts to us, God's children. We are never begging God for something we, in our goodness, would like to have for another, but which God, out of stinginess, wants to withhold! No matter how imaginative we are, no matter how broad our sympathies become, no matter how wonderful the thing which we can imagine for another, God has already thought of it before we did. We are not informing God what would be good for the child God created.

The very fact that we can get hold of some lovely idea, or vision, or gift for a child of God is simply because God let us think God's thought after him. Jesus himself said, "If you then, who are evil, know how to give good gifts to your children, how much more will your Father who is in heaven give good things to those who ask him!" (Matt. 7:11, *RSV*).

In the business of praying for another person, the first thing of importance is trust in this sort of God.

The second thing necessary is a love for people growing out of a proper concept of the nature of humanity.

It is important to see that people are not isolated units in society, but that we are all bound together. Harry Emerson Fosdick said,

> Persons are not separate individuals, merely like grains of sand
> in a bag, but, as Paul says, they are "members, one of another."
> The ganglia of a nervous system are hardly more intimately
> related and more interdependent than are the people in this
> world of ours. As Professor Everett once put it, "We ask the
> leaf, 'Are you complete in yourself?' And the leaf replies, 'No,
> my life is in the branch.' And so we ask the branch, 'Are you
> complete in yourself?' And the branch replies, 'No, my life is in
> the trunk.' And we ask the trunk, and the trunk says, 'No, my
> life is in the roots.' And we ask the roots, and the roots say,
> 'No, my life is in the trunk and the branches and the leaves.
> Keep the branches stripped of leaves and I shall die.'"[1]

This is true of the tree of personal being. We are so bound together in this closely reticulated system of interpersonal life that what we think, or what we fail to think, profoundly affects other people. The work that we do or the work that we fail to do profoundly affects other people. Is there a husband or wife who is not deeply affected by the emotions, spirituality, thinking, and the work of the chosen life partner?

Every single one of us has friends or family members who are alive today because of the medical knowledge that has come at infinite price to other people. Because of the thinking and the research of other people, those whom we love are alive.

We are touched by the affection given or withheld by another. The question often asked concerning intercessory prayer may equally apply to the giving of affection and love: "Do you mean to tell me that a child who has been deprived of genuine affection, of true agape love or understanding, will suffer serious consequences simply because he or she didn't have anyone to love him at the proper time?" The answer is that a person deprived of this sort of love often spends much of adulthood trying somehow to fill the gaps left in his or her being by that deprivation.

God is this sort of God, and life is this sort of life, and we are this sort of people. We are so knit together that we profoundly affect others by our thinking or lack of thinking, by our working or lack of working, by our praying or lack of praying, by our loving or lack of loving. This is the way God has made us.

If we are going to pray for others we have to trust in God, we must have a love of people, and we must be aware that we are bound together with them in relationships which are intimate and real.

If we can trust God and love people deeply—if we can effectively love God and effectively love people—the result is the flowering of intercessory prayer.

Prayer, the rare privilege granted to us as God's children, is the act of being the mediator between God and God's people, between this person and that person, between this group and that group.

When we are ready to come to God to pray for another, our first step is to examine our own trust in God. We must come to the place where we would prefer this person whom we love to be in God's hands rather than in our own hands. It sounds almost ludicrous to have to spell that out. But it is not quite as ludicrous as it sounds, for all too often we feel that the person will fare a little bit better if she stays in our hands! Because we are closer to her, we feel that we know her better than does God, who is a long way off. We think we can call the moves. It is difficult for us to get to the point where we really trust God enough to give our loved one over. But if we tightly hold on to the person we love, we are not really trusting God.

One of the fallacies of some of the literature on prayer is the equating of optimism with faith, never allowing us to hold negative thoughts. This is not Christian. Christians bring negative thinking, doubts, fears—bring them all to God. Having done this we trust God enough to relinquish the loved one for whom we pray. Rather than equating optimism with faith and refusing to face the alternatives and all the possibilities, we put our trust in God. We say, "God, this is the way I see it. This is what I want for this person whom I love. As I see the picture, this is what you would like; this is your will as far as I can determine it." But we must remember that we are fallible human creatures; we are weak; we are sinful. God's will may differ from our will. And so, in the final analysis we cry out, "God, this is the way I see it. Nevertheless, not my will but yours be done."

An outgrowth of this trust in God will be the alignment of our own lives with God's purposes, until God's purposes become the dominant desires of our own lives. We need not worry about the objections of those who say that our attitudes run counter to natural law and that we have no right to try to upset the balance of the universe.

What we are doing is bringing ourselves to the place where we are aligned with the eternal purposes of God. Charles George Gordon, an English Army officer and colonial administrator in the Sudan in the nineteenth century, cried one day, "God, I think I would gladly be shot tonight if I could stop this slave traffic."[2] He had come to identify himself with what he believed to be the will of God. He believed that the will of God was opposed to the slave traffic, and he was ready for his life to be snuffed out if thereby the traffic could be stopped.

John Knox one day cried, "God give me Scotland, else I die!"[3] He believed that it was the will of the Eternal God that Scotland should know Christ. And he aligned himself with that will.

Trusting God brings us to the place that, knowing we are fallible and weak, but determined to be and to do the best we can, we come to live our lives in accord with the eternal purposes of Almighty God. We say, "All right, God, here I am, available to you for the achievement of your purposes whatever those purposes may be."

What is God's purpose? God's primary purpose is to cause all things and all people to cohere in Christ. It is God's purpose to bring about community. God wants us to belong to one another. God wants the partitions to be broken down. God wants nations to be brought into a family of nations. God wants races to understand one another. God wants people to understand one another. God wants his beloved community to have a degree of love it has never known.

When we trust the God and Father of our Lord, Jesus Christ, we bring ourselves into alignment with the will of a God who has come and died upon a cross in order to win the world to this community. Then our consciousness reaches out in a yearning and a love for people, to reconcile them and mediate the agape love of God's own self to bring this community into existence.

When my consciousness reaches up to God, and when my consciousness reaches out to this person whom God loves—I yearn for them to be together. As I hold them together in my imagination, as I hold them in the orbit of my love, I am engaging in intercessory prayer.

Anyone who has never seriously prayed in intercession for another person has never known the flowering of love—has never known love in its true depths.

Notes

[1] Harry Emerson Fosdick, *The Meaning of Being a Christian* (New York: Association Press, 1964), p. 266.

[2] Harry Emerson Fosdick, *The Meaning of Prayer* (New York: Association Press, 1949), p. 174.

[3] Ibid.

Part IV

~•~

Affirming Gifts

11

Calling Forth Gifts

∾

A series of three homilies in the autumn of 1963 brought to full expression the themes of forgiveness and the calling forth of gifts that were being explored in the previous decade.

Every person called by Jesus Christ into his Body is given a gift to be employed on behalf of the whole Body. When each member's gift is being exercised, the Body will function smoothly with richness and power.

∾ *The Person as Gift* ∾

The unity and maturity of the Body are in direct ratio to the diversity or the multiplicity of the gifts in evidence within it. A congregation cannot be mature if it has only a few outstanding leaders who exercise charisma. The diversity of gifts within the community must be discovered, with each member exercising one or more gifts. The so-called lesser gifts are as significant and important as those more easily recognizable. Often there are persons who feel they do not have a gift or anything that is really needed. This is a false assumption.

In his first letter to the Corinthians, chapter 12, Paul speaks of the great variety of spiritual gifts, emphasizing that "to *each* is given the manifestation of the Spirit for the common good" (v. 7, *RSV*) and that "the Spirit apportions to *each one* individually" (v. 11, *RSV*). In other words, the gift conferred by the Holy Spirit upon a person in Christ is not a vague, general propensity but a specific power or capacity peculiar to the individual, to be exercised for the good of the group. The failure to take this teaching of Paul seriously is the cause of much of the apathy and ineffectiveness in the Christian Church today.

Each member called by God to belong to the church comes in by an experience that may take place very suddenly or over a long period of time, but it is an experience in which he or she enters into the life and death and resurrection of Jesus Christ. This is the only way we come into the Body of Christ—we live our way into it, with all that this implies.

Paul says that if a person is in Christ, old things have passed away; all things become new. He is saying that the whole basis upon which we operate is different—an unbelievably radical change takes place. Our values and the way we view life change. Our whole motivational system is new.

First of all, we are freed from the horrible burden of viewing life as demand, as "oughtness," as duty, as obligation, and from the unspeakable pressure of trying to meet the demand. Instead, we see life as gift. To accept, to know the love of Jesus Christ, is to see life as gift, to see it as grace, to see it as feast, as banquet, because Jesus Christ is the gift of God. Thanks be to God for his unspeakable gift! For God so loved the world that he gave his only begotten son.

Next, we are freed from the unconscious but very constant attempt to atone for our inability to live up to the demands which press in upon us. We know we are not faithful in living up to these demands, and we keep trying to make atonement—often subtly and sometimes in ways not so subtle. Christ comes primarily as savior, not as accuser. A life with Jesus Christ becomes one of praise, of gratitude, expectancy, freedom, excitement, wonder, newness, and a feeling of "What gift will be bestowed upon me today?" rather than wondering what will be required of me today.

All of this is the result of the gift of the Holy Spirit, which takes place in the very depths of our being. I have a feeling that the people who talk most freely about this new birth are the ones who understand it least. A unique self begins to emerge. That which was there, though imprisoned, begins to break forth. That illusive thing we call the self begins to take shape. That winsomeness which shone through only in spots, recognizable only by those of special discernment, comes through now more strongly, consistently, and is visible to many more people. We become free enough, safe enough, for unique traits (endearing traits that possibly only a discerning parent ever saw, and that have been lost somewhere along the way) to emerge again. Our essential, true selves, which were tied up, traumatized, imprisoned, begin to come forth.

This new birth does not impose on the personality something that is alien to it; rather, it brings into actuality, into fullness, that which was always there—those sensitive feelings, those yearnings, those tastes, that more tender dimension of our natures which somehow has always embarrassed us. One day we become aware that we are no longer afraid of that tender dimension. New strengths begin to emerge, new consistencies, new capacities, new humilities. A mysterious new being is being fashioned, and at the heart of this becoming is the divine action. This mystery we call the Holy Spirit. Jesus Christ is at work making us fully human. He is bringing into being the new humanity, ready to be a part of the new creation, to live with God eternally.

Christ makes each of us something unlike any other creation ever fashioned by God—something wonderful, exciting, unique; something specifically needed in the total Body of Christ. This uniqueness, this very self that is so hard to describe, this charismatic person, this gift to us from the Holy Spirit is the primary gift that we bring to the Body. Without it the Body would be immeasurably impoverished.

∾ *Calling Forth the Gifts of Others* ∾

Since the calling forth of uniqueness is a mission of God, it seems self-evident that this is our primary mission as Christians. We are to call forth the gifts of other people, to set them free, to throw the lifeline to them, and to be the ones who, under God, help a person discover that for which he or she was created.

The question is, how to call forth the gifts in others? It is amazing how long we can be with people and not call forth any of their gifts. In fact, we often do just the opposite. But to love people means to help them recognize their uniqueness and to discover their gifts.

In freedom. We begin to be really helpful in calling forth the gifts of others when we understand and employ our own charisma, when we ourselves are functioning in freedom, when our "oughtness" is eliminated and we are having the time of our lives doing what we want to do. The genuineness of our freedom is easily discernible. Children discern their charisma, their uniqueness, as it unfolds, when mothers enjoy being mothers and fathers enjoy being fathers. They are seeing parenthood as a gift, not as a demand. Without the exercise of the parents' gift, the gift of the child is not drawn forth. One of the difficulties of family life is too much "oughtness," too much demand, too much keeping the machinery going.

The counseling of another is effective only to the extent that we employ this skill in freedom, not helping the other person merely because we feel we should. Preaching and teaching are effective when they are free, spontaneous, and cheerful, rather than some sort of exhibitionism. A protective coating of false gaiety and cheerfulness is difficult to bear. But a genuine cheerfulness is a form of faith and is a corollary of the free exercise of one's own gifts.

Jesus said, "In the world you have tribulation." You are going to be up against all sorts of things, but "be of good cheer, I have overcome the world" (John 16:33, *RSV*). He said this to person after person. He didn't mean "Cheer up!" in the superficial, saccharine way we often do. The cheerfulness Jesus was talking about is a characteristic of a person who exercises his or her charisma in freedom.

All of us had best find out what we really want to do and start doing it, with whatever it involves. If you have to give up your responsibility, give it up; if the church goes to pieces, so be it. But we must find what we really want to do because nothing else is going to help anybody.

In detachment. In calling forth the gifts of others, somehow we have to stop trying to control them. We have to learn something of the meaning of detachment.

Joe Knowles, a pastoral counselor with the Pastoral Counseling and Consultation Center of Greater Washington, tells this story, which illustrates detachment. During a meeting of one of his therapy groups something very exciting began to happen, but it was also very threatening. Joe started to take control of the discussion so the group would work out the right decision and the situation would not get out of hand. As he was tempted to do this, God spoke to him and said, "Joe, take your hands off the group." He obeyed for a few minutes, took his hands off, and let the group continue to move. But again he became anxious and started to get in there to control things. God spoke to him and said, "Joe Knowles, take your hands off the group." For a few minutes he obeyed, and then once more began to interfere. This time God said, "Joe Knowles, take your cotton-picking hands off that group!"

We are afraid. If we do take our hands off—what in the world might emerge? We might not like what would emerge in our husband, or wife, or friends. Our church might become something entirely different from what it is now. We are afraid to take our hands off, although, when we do not take our hands off, we wind up with what is hardly worth having. In subtle and overt ways we try to mold others, until our closest friends are in straitjackets. The Holy Spirit will work if we just release the person and let any sort of strange concoction emerge. The hardest thing in the world seems to be to stop clutching and fashioning—to release one who is meaningful to us.

In expectation. God has not created a single person whose essence and uniqueness are not eternally needed. Longing for you and for me, God will continue to reach out for us, as the shepherd searched for that one lost sheep, until we discover our charisma. When we love a person, the only way we can really take our hands off is by committing him in a new way to God's care, to God's love. Letting go is being willing to trust God for whatever strange new work may emerge in the person we release.

Something unpleasant may occur in the process of gradual release of the person who is being born anew through the power of the Holy Spirit. The real character of the new humanity is obscured for a time by the turmoil, the anxiety, the hostility, the downright hatred which also begin to emerge into consciousness. The true dimensions of the old humanity are seen for what they are. This can be a time of discouragement and despair. One sees with greater objectivity the unbelievably demonic shadows of one's life, the indifference to the spiritual, the unwillingness to take the risk of faith, the inability to love, and the ease with which we, in a thousand subtle ways, actually despise our brothers and call them fools. Even so, the new begins to emerge, and this "becoming" self is the gift of the Holy Spirit—the new self that is needed by Christ and his Body. Without it the new humanity, the new creation, will not be complete. The creation will be forever incomplete without you, without your gift. This is a staggering truth.

Out of this fundamental gift perhaps many gifts will emerge. There will be many functions, though they will change from time to time. There will be motherhood, fatherhood, teaching, preaching, administration, healing. Then the time will come when we no longer exercise certain gifts, perhaps because of illness or old age; but we will still belong to the Body, even more deeply than we do now, because we are grafted more deeply into it. The primary gift is the gift of the person, regardless of his or her function.

We have said that the primary mission of the Christian is to call forth this gift from others—the gift of the Holy Spirit. This is the good news. We are not sent into the world in order to make people good. God forbid! We are not sent to encourage them to do their duty. People have so resisted the Gospel because we have imposed new burdens upon them rather than calling forth their gifts. We are to let people know that God is for them. We are to let them know that they are not doomed to an existence that is less than fully human. God is calling them into the family of God's love; their uniqueness forms a part of the whole. God is a gracious God, who has already judged the earth in mercy in Jesus Christ. The good news is that people can be what in their deepest hearts they know they were intended to be, and they can do what they were meant to do. As Christians we are heralds of these good tidings.

Becoming ourselves. The charismatic person is one who, by her very being, will be God's instrument in calling forth gifts. The person who is having the time of her life doing what she is doing has a way of calling forth the deeps of another. Such a person is herself good news. She is the embodiment of the freedom of the new humanity. Verbal proclamation of the good news becomes believable. The person who exercises her own gift in freedom can allow the Holy Spirit to do in others what the Spirit wants to do.

Our problem is that we resist receiving the gift of God's very life, and we also resist receiving the gift of another. It is much easier to love in a moralistic sense, or to do something for another person, than it is genuinely to love and care for the person, to call forth the gift. To call forth another's gift is to love her as she is; to want her to be what and who she is at the given moment, no matter what and who she is. But most often we do not want or seek God—or the essence of the person.

Through discipline. Our discipline of prayer is a channel by which we receive the gift of God's very being. Not merely a rule that we keep—this is a time when we become still—a time when we let God address us, command us, penetrate us, exercise sovereignty over us. It is a time when we are addressed and we respond; a time of dialogue, of actually receiving the gift of God. The trouble we have setting aside this time for prayer and making it a basic, vital point of our lives says something about our resistance to the gift of God. We say we have trouble with our disciplines when actually we do not want God to get too close.

For long centuries God has spoken to his people in a unique way through the Scriptures. In the Living Word God actually comes to us— not merely through our reading of a book, or the keeping of a rule. Why do we have trouble with it? Because we have trouble receiving the gift of God's very life.

The same thing is true of worship, the time when we are open to the living God. We come to receive God. No telling what would hap- pen to us if we conceived worship in its proper terms as the time when the living God is present in our midst. Who knows what might happen if we, as a people, really believed this!

To be part of a fellowship group or a mission group simply means that God speaks to us when we are bound together in a disciplined covenantal community. God comes to us through people—through the community of faith. Again, we have trouble at the point of yielding our lives, being obedient to one another.

The discipline of giving is our response to the desperate and poor of the world. As a symbol of our trust in God's provision for us, our giving opens the channels so that God can come. We do not hold on to our own security. But again we seem to say, "God, don't come too close."

Through Jesus Christ. Let us keep clearly in mind the fact that God gives the gift of himself to humanity through Jesus Christ. Our very resistance to Jesus—the concrete gift of God given to us—also says something about our fear of God. So often we feel that God the Father/Mother and God the Holy Spirit are sufficient; God the Son is a confusing extra. We do not quite know what to do with him, although it is through Christ that God gives himself to us and enters into covenant relation with humanity.

Our freeing takes place through the gift of Jesus Christ. Our own uniqueness emerges as we accept him as Savior, as Lord, as Master. But at this point of concreteness we hesitate, we argue, we wait. In Jesus Christ there is no abstraction which allows us to remain in control of our own destiny. Here is one who comes in the form of a servant, who comes giving his life to the uttermost, who comes dying on a cross. Here is one who comes on our behalf for our reconciliation, as our redeemer, claiming our total allegiance. He gives himself totally to us and asks that we give ourselves totally to him.

When we are open to this gift, all of life is thrown into a new orbit. We know intuitively that it is a great risk to accept this gift. We know that if we are open to it, if we are open to him who is Sovereign Lord, we shall be profoundly changed. We are not dealing with an abstraction; we are dealing with God, who is incarnate in human history, who comes to us as a Person. So we ask the question, "What will happen if I do let him come in, if I accept him as Lord? What will I be like when he is done with me?"

Through risk. Most of us want to change at those points where our present unhealthy responses to life cause us pain. At the same time we want to hold on to much of the way we are put together. If we accept this gift of God, the gift of his own life, we cannot remain what we have been; we will become a new creation. The problem is largely one of willingness to take risk, of letting our images of ourselves go, of risking what will happen when God actually breaks into human life and begins to work in the depths of our beings. We take the risk, not knowing what will emerge, not knowing what kind of person we will become.

Somehow, there has to be the faith and the trust that what we will become will be right because God is doing it. At this point the church, when it has been true to itself, has for two thousand years continued to proclaim Jesus Christ as Savior and Lord of life. The church says that with personal acceptance of Jesus Christ, when we accept the gift of God in the concreteness of his Son, we begin to participate in the new humanity.

To resist Jesus Christ is really to resist the very essence of God—to resist who and what God is—to ask God to be someone God is not. This we do so often to one another: before I accept you, you must be something that you are not; you must be what I would like you to be. We make this same demand of God.

Agape love. In all the foregoing we have been trying to come to grips with the nature of love, and we have found it is not as easy as we thought. The word most frequently used for Christian love is *agape*. The noun is used approximately 120 times in the New Testament and, in its verbal form, more than 130 times.

Why did the New Testament writers discard the other words for love and use the word *agape* almost exclusively? For one thing, *eros* was used most often in connection with lust. And rather than *philia,* according to Barclay, Christians needed a more inclusive word. Agape love demands the exercise of the whole person to all people—those who are nearest and dearest, to those who love us, to those who are in the Christian fellowship, to neighbor, to enemy, to the world. This kind of love has to do primarily with the mind, with the principle by which we deliberately live, and with the will. Agape is the power to love the unlovable. It is the power to love people we do not like.

Jesus commands us to love our enemies in order to be like God. We are not told to love in order to win our enemies or to get results, but that we may be children of the Father, who sends his rain on the just and the unjust, who looks after both the good and the evil. The predominant characteristic of this agape love is that, no matter what a person is like, God seeks nothing but his or her highest good. As an unconquerable benevolence, an invincible good will taking the initiative, agape is an activity of the whole person toward the other person.

Willing the highest good is a very general sort of thing. But it is also specific, for it provides an atmosphere in which other persons exercise their own uniqueness in freedom so that they become alive. They become fully human and what God intended when they were created. Loving in this sense has to do with the whole way we are put together and the way we respond as human beings. Not merely something we do as a matter of principle—not simply a rule—it is a way of life.

The universality of love. Love has to do with the way we see life and people and their meaning. The Christian sees people betrothed to God through Jesus Christ. This is shocking. God is betrothed to all human-kind, regardless of what we are like, so all humankind is potentially in Jesus Christ. Each of us can respond, but God is married to us whether we respond or not. It's ridiculous! It's absurd! The scandal of the Gospel!

Agape love is not something fitful or spotty. In a sense it is not at all selective. How does it use discretion concerning the particularity of loving? How do I give the gift of myself? How do I give the gifts which express myself to a particular person? In this sense love has to use discretion, but in another sense it is not selective at all; it just reaches out to every person and every combination of persons with no exclusiveness or discrimination. The rain falls on the just and the unjust, and God looks after the evil and the good.

If there are people we tend to exclude—people for whom we do not desire good, happiness, joy, fullness of being, the fullness of humanity; or if there is any combination of people, any segment of humanity, no matter how cruel and how harmful one segment may be to another or how much an enemy one segment is to another—if we are not for all segments and all people, then this agape has not broken for us.

So often we say, "Yes, I am for him, but . . . " "I am for her, but . . . " This "but" is more powerfully heard than the part about our being for the person or willing his or her good. We will have to eliminate the "but." No matter what his problem, no matter how difficult they are, I'm for this person or this group. I will affirm, protect, encourage, and I shall not be bothered in the slightest by "guilt by association" or "contempt by association" because I stand alongside. I will maintain a close identification with all persons.

The particularity of love. In addition to the universality of love there is also a particularity which is important. Certain people are given to us for a continuing, more costly involvement; we do not select them. To be with these people in this way, to recognize this givenness, means a much more threatening self-revelation, an opening up in ways that leave us with a sense of awe. In the presence of the inwardness of another, the uncovering of another, we are on holy ground.

The universality and the particularity must be kept in the right creative tension. Both are important. The universality must prepare us for the particularity, and the particularity for the deeper thrust into the life of all humankind. Otherwise we experience that fatal twist: in loving all humankind we will love no one deeply or, in seeking to love one person, we will love him or her exclusively and neglect the rest of the human race.

The risk of love. Another aspect of agape love involving faith is the matter of risk-taking. In loving we encounter enormous risk. We must be willing to have something emerge in the beloved that is quite different from what we could predict. We have not been given the capacity to see completely what another will be when his or her gift is fully known or exercised. To employ our imaginative gift is fun as we reach out in love to another, but the outlines of what we picture must be held rather loosely because God will call forth unimaginable newness, genuine uniqueness. And who can picture uniqueness which has not yet materialized?

I talked recently to a friend concerning two possible paths as he made his search for God. One involved participation in the life of this community, its worship, and its more formal phases. The other did not involve being a part of this particular church. As we talked, I suggested that either course was all right with me and would not affect my love for him. "I know you mean that," he responded, "but I can't under-stand its being all right with you either way." It has to be all right either way, because we do not know what path really leads to the uniqueness of the person. Part of our difficulty lies at the point of risk-taking. If I love this person unreservedly, if my love in some way calls forth his gift, will the person give himself to me when he has the whole world to choose from? Perhaps we have chosen each other in great immaturity and mutual need. If this person becomes a free, charismatic person, perhaps I will not be in the running at all. Sometimes the opposite is true, and he may choose me and I do not want him to choose me. Risk-taking is always involved.

Love requires faith in God. I have to know that God is gracious and can be trusted. God is for me. God can be counted on to "grow me up" into the fullness of the stature of Jesus Christ. God has chosen me, and "if God is for us, who can be against us?" God is faithful and what God is producing in the other person can be trusted not to restrict me. The very act of loving is a freeing thing and we need not fear what God will do to us through the one whom we love.

The sacrifice of love. Love is two things: seeing and risk-taking. But there is a further very important issue: the transition from not loving to loving, from being powerless to call forth the gift of another to becoming the channel of this miracle—the miracle of having aliveness occur in another because God has loved through us and reached into the depths of another through us. What is in this transition? What does it involve? We usually assume that if the person is loved she will be loving; if he has been made secure he will make other people secure. We assume that the more love a person receives the more he has to give, and the more security she has, the more she can be depended on to give others a sense of security.

Dr. Peter Bertocci, professor of philosophy at Boston University, seriously questions this sequence. He says there is a deeper question to consider here. When I receive love, or understanding, or security, I am a relatively passive participant. The other person doing the thinking, the imagining, the giving, the actual loving is experiencing whatever creativity is involved. To move from being loved to doing the loving is radical and calls for a new conception of myself. How does this happen? What is it that happens? In essence it is an emotional experience of knowing Jesus Christ.

The source of love. How do you let Jesus Christ in? How does he begin to talk with you? He is the source of love; you simply cannot do this kind of loving on your own. It is not natural! Loving involves faith and relationship with Jesus Christ, who is the gift of God's love. In holy communion we receive this gift.

Do not let anything stop your seeking with all your heart and mind and soul intimate relationship with the Person Jesus. This relationship is the key to transition from being loved to being able to love. Some of us have been greatly loved through the years, and we still do not know how to love in this way. Some of us have had as much security as people ever have, but we don't spend our lives giving other people a sense of security. On the other hand, there are some people who have had no security at all—some who have not been loved. Yet they are able to give love in a way that they have never humanly received it, because of this strange miracle that takes place within the human soul—the miracle of a living relationship with Jesus Christ.

12

Called to Be Prophets

∼

One of the founding principles of The Church of the Saviour is the encouraging and developing of the ministry of the laity. In 1979, after the separation of the church into six faith communities, Gordon called for a full expression of the prophetic voice.

Living as we are in the waning years of this century, let us consider three ways in which Christian communities might be strengthened.

First. Our leadership, which is now disillusioned and tougher than it used to be, could become a less busy leadership with much more leisure. With that new leisure would come a new tenderness and sweetness combined with toughness.

Second. We would learn what it means to be a prophetic people, a people who are prophets.

Third. We would emphasize and strengthen the whole healing dimension of community. This is happening here and there, but healing is not an area in which we are especially strong.

Concerning the second area, prophecy, the pertinent Scripture is found in the forty-ninth and fiftieth chapters of Isaiah, and the fourteenth chapter of 1 Corinthians.

First, from Isaiah 49:

> Listen to me, you coasts and islands,
>   pay heed, you peoples far away:
>   from birth the LORD called me,
>   he named me from my mother's womb.
> He made my tongue his sharp sword
>   and concealed me under cover of his hand;
>   he made me a polished arrow

and hid me out of sight in his quiver.
He said to me, "You are my servant,
  Israel through whom I shall win glory";
    so I rose to honour in the LORD's sight
  and my God became my strength.
Once I said, "I have labored in vain;
I have spent my strength for nothing, to no purpose";
    yet in truth my cause is with the LORD
      and my reward is in God's hands.
And now the LORD who formed me in the womb to be his
      servant,
  to bring Jacob back to him
  that Israel should be gathered to him,
  now the LORD calls me again:
  it is too slight a task for you, as my servant,
  to restore the tribes of Jacob,
    to bring back the descendants of Israel:
  I will make you a light to the nations,
  to be my salvation to earth's farthest bounds. (vv. 1–6)

Isaiah 50:

The Lord GOD has given me
    the tongue of a teacher
    and skill to console the weary
    with a word in the morning;
    he sharpened my hearing
that I might listen like one who is taught.
    The Lord GOD opened my ears
and I did not disobey or turn back in defiance.
  I offered my back to the lash,
    and let my beard be plucked from my chin,
I did not hide my face from spitting and insult;
  but the Lord GOD stands by to help me. (vv. 4–7)

1 Corinthians, chapter 14, immediately follows the thirteenth chapter, which is perhaps the most beautiful description of the meaning of love in the English language. When that chapter ends we usually stop reading. The fourteenth chapter begins this way: "Put love first," which is the command having to do with the thirteenth chapter; it continues, "but there are other gifts of the Spirit at which you should aim also, and above all prophecy" (v. 1).

If anyone speaks in tongues he is talking with God, not with men and women; no one understands him, for he speaks divine

mysteries in the Spirit. On the other hand, if anyone prophesies, he is talking to men and women, and his words have
power to build; they stimulate and they encourage. Speaking in
tongues may build up the speaker himself, but it is prophecy
that builds up a Christian community. I am happy for you all to
speak in tongues, but happier still for you to prophesy. The
prophet is worth more than one who speaks in tongues—unless
indeed he can explain its meaning, and so help to build up the
community. Suppose, my friends, that when I come to you I
speak in tongues: what good shall I do you unless what I say
contains something by way of revelation, or enlightenment, or
prophecy, or instruction?" (1 Cor. 14:1–6, paraphrased)

We do not decide what constitutes the essence of God's authentic
servant people. God's word clearly spells this out. And we have the
power to accept it or reject it. Either we play games with ourselves,
calling our body a servant body when in reality it is not; or we constantly struggle to close the gap between who we are in our dullness
and sinfulness, and who the faithful, authentic servant is as understood
by divine revelation. These are the choices we have.

The notion of the servant of Yahweh in the Old Testament is picked
up, fulfilled, and completed in the New Testament—conceived initially
and ideally as the whole nation; later as a segment or remnant of the
nation; and then awaited as an individual. Always included as basic to
this notion is prophecy. The service rendered by the servant always
included speaking the word of Yahweh, although speaking did not
include the whole service. Prophecy is the word of the Lord. Speaking
is a special form of action which will accomplish what no other form of
action will accomplish. "[My word] shall not return to me fruitless" (Isa.
55:11).

All of the descriptions concerning the servant were fulfilled in Jesus
of Nazareth. He was the word of God made visible. He in his own
being was the word; he was the incarnate word. All the words that he
spoke were the words of the Father. If he said it, the Father said it.
Jesus said, "I don't do anything on my own."

Then, in Jesus, God began to gather a new nation, the New Israel, a
new people, Christ's body, the church. This new nation was at last able
to do what the old nation was never able to do. Through Christ's death
and resurrection, God released the Holy Spirit in unprecedented
Pentecostal power to reside in the people. The people were now
empowered to do what all along they had been intended to do: to be

an authentic servant people living amid all the nations until Yahweh's justice, righteousness, and peace would become the accepted way of all of the nations of humankind.

Seen in the biblical light we are now the servant people with a clear commission. We cannot tamper with the nature of the servanthood; it is clearly given. The nature of who we are is one of the clearest things in Scripture. We are a nation of prophets, and each one of us, as part of our belonging to Jesus Christ, is to render the service of prophetic speech. We are all called to this form of action. Easy to describe, this role is extremely difficult to grasp and accept emotionally. The tendency is to shift the responsibility for prophecy to those very few in whom it is obviously developed. Perhaps it will always be more developed in some than in others. But each of us must speak the very word of the Lord, which means that each of us must be a prophet.

Obvious deterrents to speaking the word of the Lord are the inevitable suffering and possible death that always accompany the way of the prophet. The mere utterance of truth can arouse anger in some people. A history of the martyrs reveals the sourness, wickedness, malignity, and ferocity of which the hearts of humans are capable. Thus it always was in Israel, a nation not only of prophets but also of slayers of prophets. According to Christ, prophet-slaying was the ineradicable habit of Israel. He says, "You are the sons of the men who killed the prophets. . . . O Jerusalem, Jerusalem, the city that murders the prophets and stones the messengers sent to her!" (Matt. 23:31, 37). To the prophets who bear it, the word of God has always brought reproach, estrangement, indignities, torments, and sometimes death.

Up to the time of Isaiah, who wrote in the latter part of the sixth century, there had been the following notable suffering for the word: Among the martyrs who suffered Elijah was always mentioned. Then there were Micaiah, the son of Imlah, and Isaiah—first Isaiah—if the story is true that he was slain by Manasseh. And later, more lonely and heroic than all, came Jeremiah, a laughingstock, a mockery, reviled, smitten, fettered, condemned to death. Jeremiah said, "I rue the day that I was born. I wish the person who brought the news to my father, saying that a manchild had been born, had never brought the news!" (Jer. 20:14–15, paraphrased).

In words which recall the experience of so many individual Israelites, Isaiah describes his martyrdom in immediate consequence of his prophecy in this way: "I was not rebellious, I turned not backward. I gave my back to the smiters, and my cheeks to those who pulled out the beard; I hid not my face from shame and spitting" (Isa. 50:5–6, RSV). Such was the reward with which obdurate Israel met her prophets, the inevitable martyrdom which followed their uttering of God's word.

Jesus' suffering fell upon him because he was a prophet. He was more than a prophet, but his suffering fell upon him because he was a prophet. He argued explicitly that he must suffer because the prophets before him had suffered. He put himself in the line of the martyrs. As they had killed the servants who had preceded him, he said, so would they kill the Son. His enemies sought to entangle him in his talk; because of his talk they brought him to trial. Jesus submitted to suffering for the word's sake—the essential obligation which lies upon the true prophet. Prophecy, then, equals suffering and often death.

The reluctance to name and cultivate the prophetic dimension of servanthood is surely understandable. But the very clear word—which is difficult for us to grasp—is that each of us is to learn to speak the word of the Lord. "He made my tongue his sharp sword" (Isa. 49:2). Your tongue is to be his sharp sword.

The word of the Lord is penetrating and confronting and disturbing, always coming into the order of selfishness from the realm of God's own being. The way we have organized our society is fundamentally different from the way in which God conceives it, and the way in which God's own being longs for it to be ordered. When we speak the word of the Lord, we are speaking it from his realm, from his being, penetrating that realm which is organized in a selfish way completely contrary to God's justice. Ours is to be the word of light penetrating darkness; the word of justice penetrating all unjust social arrangements; the word of judgment in every arrangement not in consonance with the nature of God's eternal love.

Each of our tongues is to be God's sharp sword speaking in that penetrating, threatening, warning, and thus saving way. We all need to speak that word and let it come crashing into this existing order from the only order that will eternally abide. Those of the world who do not repent will be furious. But we will have been obedient. Again, as the prophet says, "I was not rebellious, I turned not backward. I gave my back to the smiters" (Isa. 50:5–6, RSV). Speak the word and give your back to the smiters. That is the formula.

You say, "I'm not good at speech. I don't talk well." All of us are speaking constantly. Speech is one of the fundamental characteristics of human beings. What matters is not whether we speak, but whether we speak in ways which are mundane, idle, useless, and boring, or whether we speak the word of the Lord and thus are prophetic.

Another dimension of prophecy—another way the word breaks through us from God to his people—is in the word of consolation to the weary. Jesus said, "Come unto me all ye that labor and have too much to do, and I will give you rest"(Matt. 11:28, paraphrased). That rest from Jesus to his burdened followers and those who are not yet his followers will often be the word from him through you. The spirit of the other will be comforted; your word will literally be the word of the Lord for the comfort of the other.

Often the word of the Lord spoken through you will be a word of hope. Your word will not be that of impending judgment because of man's injustice; but you will cry out as the prophet did in approximately 540 B.C., to the exiles in Babylon, who had been there for sixty years:

> Comfort, comfort my people;
> —it is the voice of your God;
> speak tenderly to Jerusalem,
> and tell her this,
> that she has fulfilled her term of bondage,
> that her penalty is paid;
> she has received at the LORD's hand
> double measure for all her sins. (Isa. 40:1–2)

The prophet is saying to Israel in exile, "Your bondage is over, your time of exile is ended, you're going home."

Think of the time when God will give you that kind of word to speak to your people. Your word may be one which describes the reality of the glorious kingdom, present now, but also barrelling down on us in such a way that people get excited about the future rather than remaining bogged down in all of the heaviness and discouragement of what now appears so visible and real. The prophet in the book of Revelation says, "Then I saw a new heaven and a new earth, for the first heaven and the first earth had vanished. . . . I saw the holy city, new Jerusalem, coming down out of heaven from God" (Rev. 21:1–2). These words of prophecy are *every* bit as real and authentic as those that question the existing order.

The word that you have to be willing to speak will threaten all the arrangements of the existing order and will disturb people mightily. As a result of your faithfulness to that word you will suffer, and you may even die.

At other times the word given you will be a word of tremendous comfort, and you will be able to console the weary and the disheartened. Sometimes you will be able to describe the vision of the future and the kingdom of God, which is bursting into the present from the future; and you will be able to describe it in such a way that it will touch the depths of the hearts of human beings and give to them a renewed and immense sense of hope. All this by your words, your speech. The church must recapture the prophetic dimension, not only in those to whom it seems to come naturally, but in all the people. To let a fraction of the people speak the word and become wise would be unfair. All of us are to speak the word, to be bearers of the witness.

The true prophet, as opposed to the false prophet, always bathes his or her life in solitude. In the stillness the word of God is most often given. You say, "I don't have any word for the people. I don't have any word for my community. I don't even have a word for my family." But the word of God is heard in the stillness.

Thomas Merton says, "Contemplation . . . is awakening, enlightenment and the amazing intuitive grasp by which love gains certitude of God's creative and dynamic intervention in our daily life."[1] In contemplation we are "carried away by Him into His own realm, His own mystery, and His own freedom."[2] We touch a realm which is different from this realm in which people live; and in that stillness the Word leaps down from heaven, touches our spirits in the solitude, and we are given a Living Word. "It is a pure and virginal knowledge, poor in concepts, poorer still in reasoning, but able, by its very poverty and purity, to follow the Word wherever He may go."[3] We are able to break loose and speak a word against the order in which we have been drawing our paycheck and finding our security.

The problem is that it is extremely difficult for us to be prophetic in the institutions we serve. Our government institutions must be brought to see themselves as they are. For us to look at the military—see it as it really is and still serve it if we are called upon to serve—poses a real problem. To be aware of how totally wrong are the principles governing the institution that we have loved and served and in which we have found our security is to find that security threatened. In solitude we are enabled to break loose from that dependence, and are able to criticize that which we love—an extremely difficult thing to do.

We must somehow transcend every belonging in order to speak from a realm which is a different realm—the realm of God. That is what it means to be prophetic. We must break loose from these securities, and we must speak the truth as we see it. Truth is the only thing which will abide. We have to transcend every institution to which we belong, and every segment of society of which we are a part. The power to do these things is given in the solitude. You can do it. I can do it. We can begin to speak that word.

Sometimes we will speak a word of judgment, and sometimes it will be, "Comfort ye, comfort ye, my people. Your warfare is ended, your exile is over; the terms of your bondage have been fulfilled. You're going home." In the solitude you will be shown which it is. If you give the people comfort when there is no comfort to be given, you are a false prophet. And if you hold over them judgment when you should be giving them comfort, you are a false prophet. Every one of us who professes to be a Christian, who is a follower of Jesus Christ, is called to prophesy. You cannot shirk this privilege you have been given. To prophesy is your joy; it is your pain. Thank God for this part of what it means to be one of his servant people.

In a time of stillness and solitude it would be well to pray:

> Our Father, we speak when we haven't been spoken to, and out of our lives have poured chitchat on top of chitchat, inanities on top of inanities, things which are dull and boring and meaningless.
>
> But when your Son came down our human way, every word he spoke was a word from the Father, and everything he did was an action rendered to the Father and by the Father's command. Now we say that Christ lives in us, and he is the hope of glory for us individually, corporately. We would so deepen our belonging to him and so put down our roots into that stillness that every action will be a guided divine action, and every word we say will be a word of the Lord that is prophetic.
>
> Forgive us for our past; forgive me for my past, for my unfaithfulness. And come close to me and let me come close to you. Let all of us come so close that you will hide us in the palm of your hand, and you will place us in the secret place of your quiver so that we shall be polished arrows ready to be used by you in any moment, in any event.

I would dedicate myself to you this day, and I would become your prophet. In the stillness now I would listen for that word you would speak to me. In Christ's name. Amen.

Notes

¹ Thomas Merton, *New Seeds of Contemplation,* Copyright © 1972 by the Abbey of Gethsemane, p. 5. Reprinted by permission of New Directions Publishing Corp.
² Ibid.
³ Ibid.

13

Called to Be Creative

~

In 1986 Gordon addressed creativity as a gift given to us and also as the fruit that we bear.

Many of the stories in the New Testament—in the teaching of Jesus—are about fish. The disciples, for the most part, were fishermen. In the early church Christ himself was likened to the fish. In psychological parlance the great fish is a symbol for the content of the unconscious, that is, for totality.

The sixth chapter of Mark tells the story about the disciples' rejoining Jesus after having gone out two by two on their mission to call the people to repentance. They wanted to report all that they had done and taught, and to share with Jesus their grief about the death of John the Baptist, who had been beheaded by Herod. They had all felt very close to John, and they needed time to grieve—to work with the meaning of this sad event. Jesus said something very revealing to them. "Come away by yourselves to a lonely place, and rest a while" (Mark 6:31, *RSV*).

Interesting that Jesus felt what the disciples needed was a lonely place where they could rest quietly and deal with the meaning of John's death. Mark makes the comment, "Many were coming and going, and they had no leisure even to eat" (Mark 6:31, *RSV*). Some of you know something about having no leisure even to eat because so many are coming and going.

Accordingly, they set off privately by boat for a lonely place; but many saw them leave, recognized them, and went around by land hurrying from all the towns toward that place and arrived there first. So they did not have the retreat that Jesus wanted them to have, their time to rest. Instead of getting upset, when Jesus came to shore his heart went out to the people, because they were like sheep without a shepherd, and he had much to teach them. Instead of saying, "Oh, mercy. Here they are again," his heart went out to them and he began to teach them (Mark 6:32–35, paraphrased).

> As the day wore on, his disciples came up to him and said, "This is a lonely place and it is getting very late; send the people off to the farms and villages round about, to buy themselves something to eat." "Give them something to eat yourselves," he answered. They replied, "Are we to go and spend twenty pounds on bread to give them a meal?" "How many loaves have you?" he asked; "Go and see." They found out and told him, "Five, and two fishes also." He ordered them to make the people sit down in groups on the green grass, and they sat down in rows, a hundred rows of fifty each. Then, taking the five loaves and the two fishes, he looked up to heaven, said the blessing, broke the loaves, and gave them to the disciples to distribute. He also divided the two fishes among them. They all ate to their hearts' content; and twelve great basketfuls of scraps were picked up, with what was left of the fish. Those who ate the loaves numbered five thousand men. (Mark 6:35–44)

Some women and children were very likely there, too.

> As soon as it was over he made his disciples embark and cross to Bethsaida ahead of him, while he himself sent the people away. And after taking leave of them, he went up the hill-side to pray. It grew late and the boat was already well out in the water, while he was alone on the land. Somewhere between three and six in the morning, seeing them laboring at the oars against a head-wind, he came towards them, walking on the lake. He was going to pass them by; but when they saw him walking on the lake, they thought it was a ghost and cried out; for they all saw him and were terrified. But at once he spoke to them: "Take heart. It is I; do not be afraid." Then he climbed into the boat beside them, and the wind dropped. At this they were completely dumbfounded [and then this interesting comment. Why?], for they had not understood the incident of the loaves; their minds were closed. (Mark 6:45–52)

On to the eighth chapter.

> Then the Pharisees came out and engaged him in discussion. To test him they asked him for a sign from heaven. He sighed

deeply to himself and said, "Why does this generation ask for a sign? I tell you this: no sign shall be given to this generation." With that he left them, re-embarked, and went off to the other side of the lake.

Now they had forgotten to take bread with them [and all of this is following the account in the early part of chapter eight of the feeding of the four thousand with seven loaves and a few fish]; they had no more than one loaf in the boat. He began to warn them: "Beware," he said, "be on your guard against the leaven of the Pharisees and the leaven of Herod." [So they began to talk among themselves about having no bread. Knowing this, he said to them] "Why do you talk about having no bread? Have you no inkling yet? Do you still not understand? Are your minds closed? You have eyes; can you not see? You have ears; can you not hear? Have you forgotten? When I broke the five loaves among five thousand, how many basketfuls of scraps did you pick up?" "Twelve," they said. "And how many when I broke the seven loaves among four thousand?" They answered, "Seven." He said to them, "Do you still not understand?" (Mark 8:11–21).

Amazing, the sort of dialogue that went on with his disciples.

We are approaching the end of the Christian year. In several weeks we will be going into Advent, which is the beginning of another cycle. We always start with the announcement and then go to the birth; from the birth we move toward the death, and from the death to the resurrection; and from the resurrection to Pentecost; then follows a period of time to consolidate the fruits of the Spirit and to enter into that sort of creativity which issues from the resurrection and Pentecost.

The fruit of what is to happen as we live in and through the Christian year is creativity. You will bear much fruit. You will become exceedingly creative. "A grain of wheat remains a solitary grain unless it falls into the ground and dies; but if it dies, it bears a rich harvest" (John 12:24). So the end for those in Christ is infinite creativity—the true meaning of resurrection. "I came that they may have life, and have it abundantly" (John 10:10, *RSV*).

The purpose, then, of going through the Christian year is for us to enter into the death and the resurrection and the meaning of Pentecost, and to become infinitely creative, because each year we go through that cycle at ever-deepening levels.

As we are ending this period, I want to say a word about how fundamental creativity is. It is so fundamental that if you are not creative in the peculiar way that you are destined to be creative, you will be angry—deeply frustrated and angry. Quite a number of such angry people are very much in evidence.

Many people are angry—some way down deep, some not so deep. They spend a lot of energy and time trying to keep their anger within reasonable limits. Then once in a while it erupts, and often out of all proportion to the accompanying circumstances and with little reference to the poor souls that happen to be around at the moment. Of the many reasons for anger, one of the least understood and yet most important is this: the denial or blocking of creativity.

If you need to write a poem, better struggle to write it, even if you have to eat simply and live in a garret. If you need to write a book, you had better write it. If you need to create a piece of sculpture, you had better do it. If you need to build a beautiful friendship, you had better do it, even if you have to stop a lot of important things. If you need to be with your child and just love her and let her know how important she is to you and God—even if it keeps you from your promotion—you had better do it. If you need to dig in a garden and plant a seed and watch a flower grow, better do it. If you need to build institutions which will create new neighborhoods where people may flourish as in a watered garden, let nothing stop you. If you need to sing a song, sing. If you need to dance, dance. Give yourself to whatever is the special area of your own creativity. And if people do not understand, then simply know that it is their problem and not yours. Know that you must do it, else you will be angry.

God is a creator. God's being, God's life is the source of all that is. God is constantly bringing into being that which was not, that which is new. Newness is constantly breaking forth in God, through God. The flow of energy in life continues. The flow is limitless—will never give out. Coming from the limitless depths of God's being, the flow is infinite, inexhaustible. So you don't have to husband your resources and dribble them out. You can be lavish and prodigal. You will be embarrassed by the new riches being poured into your life. Jesus was so aware of the immeasurable richness of God's grace that he could only ask, "Why are you so anxious, wondering 'What we shall eat, what we shall drink?'" Don't you know there is a limitless flow of life— a superabundance of love and caring? You simply cannot exhaust it. It may be tough learning how to touch that current, how to get into that stream, to feel the flow and the power of it, to be carried by it, but one thing is certain: the stream is there. And it is limitless.

Jesus on that first Easter breathed on his disciples and said "Receive the Holy Spirit" (John 20:23). And in that moment they were in the stream of inexhaustible life. One receives the Holy Spirit by surrendering the ego to Jesus, who is then discovered deep within. He who surrenders that narrow ego, who loses his life, is the one who will find it.

John Sanford says: "The life of the kingdom is dynamic and continually evolving. This is the inner meaning of the great catch of fish."[1]

> Jesus said to Simon, "Put out into the deep water and pay out your nets for a catch." Simon answered, "Master, we were hard at work all night and caught nothing at all; (I'm not very encouraged by what you are telling us to do) but if you say so, I will let down the nets." And when they had done this, they netted such a large number of fish that their nets began to split. So they signaled to their partners in the other boat to come and help them. This they did, and loaded both boats to the point of sinking. (Luke 5:4–7)

Fish play an unusually important role in the New Testament. When Christ feeds the multitude, it is with fish. A fish is miraculously caught to supply the tax money needed. Fish is the food Jesus eats after the resurrection.

In *Dreams: God's Forgotten Language,* John Sanford says, "Fish have had special significance as a psychological symbol. The fish . . . lurks under the surface."[2] They may be abundant, but they are hard to see. However, they may be caught by patience and skill. And when they are caught, they may be eaten and taken into oneself. The contents of the inner world are also below the surface. They too may be lifted up into consciousness and taken as food for our lives.

Creativity is a function of the inner imagination, not of the ego. The ego does not create out of itself, but gives form and expression to the creativity which comes from within. An ego out of touch with the inner world can never be creative, but only rigid, and can only mimic creativity. Creativity comes when we are in contact with the living contents of the inner world, the inner fish, and bring them to the surface and give them expression in our lives.

When the ego is willing to die ("Blessed are the poor in Spirit"), then we touch inner springs; we meet the inner Christ, and we connect with that torrent of life that we call the Holy Spirit. Jesus says, "Out of your inner life will come streams of living water." Something happens when you connect with that artesian well.

This flowing inner world may also be connected with outer events. When that connection is made, creativity is staggering—even frightening. Ira Progoff, in a work called *Jung, Synchronicity, and Human Destiny*, deals with what he calls "noncausal dimensions of human experience." We think more easily in terms of causal experience. Jung says that there is a whole other realm which is noncausal. And Progoff talks about synchronistic events. All of us have experienced them. He illustrates what he means by a synchronistic event—when one event impinges on another but is not caused by it:

> During his early years, Abraham Lincoln found himself in a very difficult, conflicting situation. He had intimations that there was a meaningful work for him to do in the world. He realized, however, that the work would require him to develop his intellect and to acquire professional skills. In conflict with these subjective feelings was the fact that in Lincoln's frontier environment, intellectual tools for professional study were difficult to come by. He had reason to believe that his hopes would never be fulfilled.
>
> One day, a stranger came to Lincoln with a barrel full of odds and ends. He said that he was in need of money, and he would be much obliged if Lincoln would help him out by giving him a dollar for the barrel. . . . The contents, he said, were not of much value. There were some old newspapers and things of that sort. But the stranger needed the dollar very badly. The story tells us that Lincoln with his characteristic kindness gave the man a dollar for the barrel even though he could not imagine any use that he would have for its contents. Sometime later, when he went to clear out the barrel, he found that it contained almost a complete edition of *Blackstone's Commentaries*. It was chance, or the synchronistic acquisition of these books, that enabled Lincoln to become a lawyer and eventually to embark on his career in politics. There was a line of continuous causality working in the life of Lincoln, stirring his intimations of destiny and filling him with despair at the thought of living in a limited and difficult environment. At the same time there was a causal continuity in the life of the stranger who came upon hard times and had to sell whatever belongings he could find for a dollar. The two lines of events had no causal connections linking them. But at a significant moment in time, they came together. This was the working of the transcausal factor in synchronicity as it brought about its unanticipated results. Lincoln's purchase of the barrel and his inadvertent acquisition of *Blackstone's Commentaries* is an instance of the occurrence of synchronistic events in the life of human beings.[3]

We can talk about this coming together of things in theological terms or we can talk about it in spiritual terms. But something happens which is very, very important. We have had it happen again and again in the life of our community. Janelle Goetcheus has a dream, shares it with others, and then a stranger comes along who fits into the picture; the two meet, and Christ House is born. Within a few weeks we will celebrate the first year of the operation of Christ House, a thirty-four-bed facility for homeless persons released from the hospital but too weak and sick to be on the streets—the coming together of things which had no causal connection.

One way of seeing creativity is touching first of all one's own inner world and there meeting Christ. "In him was life, and the life was the light of men" (John 1:4, *RSV*). We are enabled to see and respond to the outer events, the fish and the barrel, and then more fish and more barrels. And so the connections happen, if only we can see them and be open to them.

The thing that has the power to block creativity is the refusal to die. "Unless a grain of wheat falls into the earth and dies, it remains alone" (John 12:24, *RSV*). Not to die, not to be in touch with the inner world, is to be not open to the totality of the whole human family. To be looking after ourselves rather than to be open to the common wealth is to miss the surging, expansive flow of life. To live thus on the surface—to live on resources which will give out—results in weariness and exhaustion; it is to become rigid, limited, and old; to feel left out and put on the shelf of the universe, lonely and not needed. Being so self-centered also results in missing the outer events. You fail to pay the meager one dollar for the barrel, because you do not even know to buy the barrel. You fail to find the books, or to know what to do with them once they are found. Jesus said, "Whoever drinks the water that I shall give him will never suffer thirst any more. The water that I shall give him will be an inner spring always welling up for eternal life" (John 4:14).

When the Spirit and the power of God are connecting with our depths, we are open and willing to surrender our egos and our wills to Jesus of Nazareth. A whole new realm of power is released which transcends the normal categories of thinking. One of our great problems is that we keep resisting what we think we understand but the meaning of which we have only an inkling. We should remember that the disciples who were close to Jesus and had left all to follow him often had not a clue as to the meaning of what he was teaching and demonstrating to them. They could not get hold of what they had actually seen. Not only did Jesus have problems communicating this new kingdom of his to the people outside; the people he was with could not get hold of it. They were blind; they could not comprehend the significance of the message, even when they had participated in a revealing event. The opposite of faith is blindness—the inability to see. Jesus had great difficulty getting not only those on the outside to understand him; he had great difficulty getting those on the inside to understand.

Blindness is an extraordinarily great problem. This last week, Mary and I were in Louisville for a conference at my seminary. At the close of one of the question-and-answer periods, a question came, and I did not have time to think before answering. I might have come up with a "better" answer, which would have been a false answer. The question was, "What's the biggest mistake that you have made in your ministry?" Without really thinking (it came from that area where the fishes are, in the unconscious), I said, "I think the biggest problem that I've had in my ministry is blindness—seeing things too late—resulting in the terrible cost other people and I have paid because of my not seeing soon enough." Jesus was always trying to help his disciples to see the real meaning of that which he was trying to teach them.

Even after the feeding of the five thousand and the feeding of the four thousand, Jesus still had cause to ask, "Do you still not understand? Are your minds closed?" (Mark 8:17).

In the ninth chapter of Mark, when he comes down from the mountain of Transfiguration and the disciples have not been able to heal the boy, Jesus says, "What an unbelieving and perverse generation! How long shall I be with you? How long must I endure you?" (v. 19). He is talking to his disciples, because they are still uncomprehending.

In Mark 10, James and John come to him and say,

"We have a little favor to ask of you."

"What's that?"

"We want you to grant us the right to sit in state with you when you come into your kingdom."

And Jesus once again says, "You do not understand; your minds are closed. You haven't gotten hold of this kingdom that I am trying to help you to grasp" (vv. 35–38, paraphrased).

We misunderstand everything unless we understand the incident of the loaves. And what are we to understand?

When we are open and connected with Christ, the meager appearance of resources does not matter. Five loaves, two fish, seven loaves, a few fish, one loaf in the boat . . . do not matter. Because of a noncausal realm of reality, everything we need is present. God is infinitely able. We can eat to our heart's content, and there will be leftovers: twelve baskets full, seven baskets full.

But somehow we cannot get hold of it. We watch it, we participate in the events, but we still worry. We wonder about whether God is really going to be there and whether or not this thing is going to work. Jesus continues to work with those inside his inner circle, trying to help them overcome their blindness. But he knows they are missing the very essence of the kingdom. He says we have been with him all these years and are still blind and do not even know that we are blind. If we know that we are blind, then we have a chance.

> Jesus said, "I have come into this world to give sight to the sightless and to make blind those that see." The Pharisees said, "Are you talking to us? Are we blind?" And Jesus said, "You know, I wish you were blind. I wish you knew it. You would have a chance. Because you say 'We see,' you can't make it" (John 9:39–41, paraphrased).

If we really understood the significance of the incident of the loaves, the amazing creativity of Jesus who is the fish, then amazing creativity would open in us as we touch our own inner world and recognize and appreciate all of those noncausal events that occur through the power of Pentecost. Then we would no longer be terrified; we would no longer be overwhelmed. Of course, we would be on the lake with all of its dangers and its threats, but we would understand the incident of the loaves. And rather than in fear and foreboding, we would simply be waiting for the next surprise of God's extravagant abundance. Our only worry would be about who would take on the kitchen detail of cleaning up the leftovers, because that is a big job, twelve baskets full of fish. That could be messy. That is what we would be worrying about, not about whether or not the miracle would happen.

For those of us who consider ourselves "on the inside," but who feel the need to recognize more clearly the signs of the kingdom at work in our world in order to enable those on the outside to overcome their blindness, it would be helpful to pray:

Holy God, we think we've got hold of a lot of things just because we've read them again and again, but then when it comes to life, we really haven't seen it, haven't got hold of it. We are not filled with a sense of wonder because of the flow of that stream of creativity in our lives. We are not waiting expectantly for that noncausal event to take place in the outer world, because of that creativity within. We worry. We try so hard to strategize. And we are so fearful that we feel over-whelmed.

We pray that somehow in these moments the scales from our eyes may be removed and we will see. We're sorry you have so much trouble with those of us who are inside. We keep worry-ing about those who are on the outside and wish that they could see. You keep trying to get those of us who are on the inside— our members, our intern members, the ones who are closest to us—to really grasp and see it and begin to live out of this amazing level of creativity. "I have come that ye might have life and have it more abundantly." Let us not be frightened of that creativity and the responsibility that it will bring.

We would commit ourselves now anew to you, O Living Christ, knowing that you will touch the inner depths of our lives, and that the streams of living water will begin to flow in unbelievable profusion. These our prayers we would make in your name, our Lord and Savior, and for your sake. Amen.

Notes

[1] John A. Sanford, *The Kingdom Within: The Inner Meaning of Jesus' Sayings,* rev. ed. (New York: Harper Collins, 1987), p. 199.

[2] John A. Sanford, *Dreams: God's Forgotten Language* (New York: Harper Collins, 1968), pp.37-38.

[3] Ira Progoff, Ph.D., *Jung, Synchronicity, and Human Destiny: Noncausal Dimensions of Human Experience* (New York: The Julian Press, 1973), pp. 170-72.

Part V

~∽~

Overcoming Fear

14

God's Answer for Anxiety

~

In 1956 Gordon addressed the issue of anxiety as part of a series on the nature of the Christian life.

Anxiety is a condition which confronts each one of us because we have been given the freedom to accept or reject God as the very ground of our existence. This primal anxiety becomes sinful anxiety when we are plagued by guilt, and this in turn degenerates into neurotic anxiety caused by the malignant relationships we have with others.

In a deep, tragic sense, all of us are sinners and, because we are sinners, we commit sins. However, the sins are only symptomatic of "the sin." The Bible spends less time dealing with the sins than on the basic conditions from which sin springs. In one sense (and in only one sense) it makes little difference which sins one commits. Our problems have a much deeper source: a sickness, an alienation, a loneliness.

If we feel alienated from others or cut off; if there is a lost harmony within our being because we do not have the unity and holiness for which we are made; if we are torn apart within ourselves; if we are cut off from God who is the ground of our being—then, of course, what we most need are restoration, reconciliation, inner healing, "at-homeness." The Bible offers the answer to our problems. It treats of two things—the question of sin, and the answer to that question: reconciliation.

How does this reconciliation come about in Christian thinking? First, we must face the self, the real self, because this is where the problem arises. We are sinners in the very depths of our being. We are sick within. You remember what John said: "If we say we have no sin, we deceive ourselves, and the truth is not in us" (1 John 1:8, *RSV*). To recognize generally what the situation is and that help is needed is an important first step, but that is not enough. We need a more specific understanding of ourselves, a more specific understanding that comes from self-searching.

Christian self-searching requires several safeguards. It must always be done under God, who is the Father/Mother of our Lord Jesus Christ. In truth, we do not do the searching. We simply open ourselves so God can search us. As the Psalmist says, "Search me, O God, and know my heart! Try me and know my thoughts! And see if there be any wicked way in me, and lead me in the way everlasting" (Ps. 139:23–24, *RSV*).

To search oneself under God means to search oneself in the light of the primal command: "You shall love the Lord your God with all your heart, and with all your soul, and with all your mind, and with all your strength . . . [and] your neighbor as yourself" (Mark 12:30–31, *RSV*). This absolute command is the demand of God upon every human life. We are to live each moment with this sort of love of God and neighbor.

We examine ourselves not only in the light of this primal command of God. We look also at the only one who has embodied the command—Jesus Christ.

To love God with all of one's heart and with all of one's soul and with all of one's mind is to respond to God as Jesus responded to God. The deepest pain of one's life is the pain of not being a saint. The deepest need of our nature, the need which the Law does not reach, is simply to be doing the will of God. Spontaneous, abandoned, full response is the response that Jesus gave. Obedience to the command requires that same response from us.

To love one's neighbor as oneself means to spend one's life as Jesus spent his life, with open arms, with a compassionate heart—going to all lengths to bring people into the love of God and, ultimately, to be willing to die for others.

When I begin my process of self-searching, I do not have to put myself in a tub and stir it all up and just keep on stirring it up for the next twenty years. Under this command of God my objective point of reference is the obedience of the Lord Jesus Christ.

Self-searching will lead to repentance. Repentance occurs deep within the life, the heart, and the mind of a person. The word literally means "a change of thinking"—a different way of looking at life, of seeing one's need, of seeing God as the answer to the need, of seeing oneself in relation to the holiness of God. Repentance leads to confession. Repentance and confession are really the same thing. When repentance is deep enough, one simply wants to verbalize with the lips what has been sensed within the heart.

Self-searching leads to a change of heart, which we then articulate and confess. Repentance must be with one's total self, and speaking it is a part of one's total self. We will always make this confession to God, and often to one another within the Christian fellowship. Self-searching, repentance, and confession then lead to self-surrender.

Surrender is voluntarily turning oneself over into God's keeping. The voluntary nature of surrender is of vital importance, because otherwise our submission to God may occur simply because God is bigger than we are. We have lived in this moral universe long enough to know that we just cannot beat God at God's own game. And so, very reluctantly, because we cannot do anything else, we, in effect, say to God, "All right, you have the ace. Here I am. I submit to you." This then comes to be another form of tyranny.

Christianity always stresses the voluntary nature of self-surrender. For this reason we were given freedom. Not a brief cry for momentary help, this is for keeps! It is for time and eternity. We are to shift the center of life from ourselves to God, so that life becomes polarized around God.

When we begin to sense that everything in our lives is not actually revolving around this new pole, we are very regretful that we have been off center even for a moment of time, and we shift back to keep centered around God.

To say exactly the same thing in another way: The first necessity is to accept ourselves as human beings where we are. To accept ourselves as responsible, free persons, we must not resist the fact that in freedom we confront issues of life and death, and we must be willing to accept the consequences of our freedom. My decision can spell the differences between life and death, between heaven and hell, between darkness and light, between community and alienation. Sometimes we have the feeling that this simply cannot be. But the plain fact is that it can!

For this reason we are eager to believe that everything is going to turn out the same in the end. You hear the statement time and time again that we are all going to the same place; we're just going in different ways. That is one way of saying, "Let's don't face differences." The fact is that we are not all going to the same place. We are not going just by a different way; some of us are not going! According to the Bible there is a sickness unto eternal death. Believing this, a Christian becomes concerned about his or her faith.

Not only must we face the fact that we are responsible, free persons, but we must be willing to accept ourselves as we are, rather than always wanting to be someone else—somebody who has five talents or ten talents instead of one—someone who had more breaks—someone who has no sordid chapters in the past.

We have the tendency to deny ourselves by wanting to be somebody else. We cannot go back and change the past. We cannot be anybody else. We are who we are—with the wasted years, with the sordid past, sometimes neurotic, sometimes psychotic. We are just ourselves, all we can be, and we must accept ourselves as we are in the present moment.

Not only must we accept ourselves, but we must accept God as God is. God the Holy One is, in love, reaching out to us where we are at this given moment. This God of ours takes the initiative, is always reaching out. Resistance and hostility to this love were so intense that they resulted in Calvary. The cost to God was a measure of our sickness and our desperate need. Surely God did no more than was needed.

All of this is to ask—in our awareness and our struggle, in our desperate reaching out for "at homeness," in our desperate desire for healing—what do we meet? Not emptiness, not a cosmic loneliness, not futility. When in my struggle I reach out to God, I touch God reaching out to me. Sometimes we talk about our own personal outreach and what it should be. We wonder what should be the outreach of a church like ours. But we know what the outreach of God is. The ultimate outreach of God is the Christ who died on Calvary.

Paul put it like this in the third chapter of Romans: "Since all have sinned and fall short of the glory of God, they are justified by his grace as a gift, through the redemption which is in Christ Jesus, whom God put forward as an expiation by his blood, to be received by faith" (vv. 23–25, *RSV*).

Christians say that there is a real meeting of God and humanity when reconciliation takes place—when forgiveness takes place. Not just some divine fact, not just a divine command by God, but an actual meeting of God and man.

Let us consider what takes place when we meet God. God does not say, "You repent and confess and I will forgive you." When we meet God, we are in repentance and we are confessing. We must always remember that when God comes and deals with our souls, it is on God's initiative. It is God who declares me forgiven. My receiving of forgiveness is not an ethical achievement on my part. I must remember this when the Tempter comes and says, "Just a minute. You are not worthy of this sort of forgiveness." My answer comes back quick as a flash, "Of course I'm not worthy, but God is worthy." Then the Tempter says, "Wait! Don't you remember the sin that dogs your life?" And my quick response, "Why should I remember that which God no longer remembers?"

We think of Martin Luther, a sensitive soul, who struggled for much of his life to find peace and freedom. He knew how heinous his sin was in the sight of God, and he yearned for freedom and relief. One night when he was in his little cell, the Tempter came. Luther had a vision of Satan holding an armful of scrolls which he began to unroll. He said, "Martin Luther, here is the account of your life written in your own handwriting. Is this your own handwriting?" Luther had to confess that it was. Satan rolled the scrolls out one by one. Then, with a fiendish grin, he turned to leave. Luther called him back, "Wait a minute. Those things are true, but written across them all is 'FORGIVEN by the blood of his son Jesus Christ.'"

We do remember our sin. We face it. But we know forgiveness to be an action of God. As the hymn says, "Nothing in my hand I bring, simply to thy cross I cling."

"Then what becomes of our boasting?" asks Paul in Romans. It is excluded. There is nothing to boast about. What does God do in this act of forgiveness? In the Bible writers make varying statements. One says, "God heals our sins." Another says, "removes them." Others say, "puts them far away," "covers them," "lifts or takes them away," "God wipes them away," "blots them out."

We get hints in the Old Testament of what the love of God is like. Back in the eighth century B.C., we have the account of Hosea. He married a woman whose name was Gomer and she bore him three children. One night he came home and Gomer was not there. She had gone off to her false lover. After days and months had passed, God commanded Hosea, who still loved his wife, to go and buy her back. Down to the slave market he went, to where she had been sold after being deserted by her lover, and he bought her back.

An insight dawned in Hosea's heart. He said, "If a mere man can love a woman like this, surely God can continue to love us when we chase after false gods." And a light begins to break in the Old Testament, preparing us for the breaking of that light in its fullness at Golgotha.

Jesus was telling us that same truth in his story of the prodigal son. The boy, you recall, came to his father before his inheritance was due. He was not willing to wait, and he said, "Father, give me my share of the property." Taking his money, he went to a far country, and wasted his substance in riotous living. One day when he was feeding swine, he came to himself. He rehearsed a little speech, because he had determined to return home. He said to himself, "I will go to my father, and say to him, 'Father, I have sinned against God and against you; I am no longer fit to be called your son.'" He had indeed come to himself.

You understand what Jesus is trying to convey through this story. When the father, who had been watching and waiting for him all the years, saw his son he began to run down the dusty road to meet him— a most undignified action for an elderly Oriental. As he took his son in his arms, the boy began to speak, "Father, I have sinned against God and against you; I am no longer fit to be called your son."

No use finishing that speech. The father turned to his servants. "Quick! fetch a robe, my best one, put it on him; put a ring on his finger and shoes on his feet. Bring the fatted calf and kill it, and let us have a feast to celebrate the day. For this son of mine was dead and has come back to life; he was lost and is found" (Luke 15:22–24). Jesus says this is our Father's attitude toward us.

Once there was a boy in prison. He was so ashamed that he did not write to his family until he was about to be released. Then he wrote to his mother and said, "Mother, I don't know how you will feel about this. I know I have hurt you very much, and I do not know whether you can forgive me. I shall be out in a few days. On Friday I will be on the train that goes almost through our backyard. If you are able to forgive me, hang a sheet on the clothes line. If it is there, I'll get off, but if not, I'll keep on going." Of course you know what happened. Every sheet in the house was flying on the clothes line when the train went by.

Calvary says that all the sheets of God's heaven are flying. God is ready, just waiting for that alienated child to come limping back home. We do not have to bring anything in our hands. We do not have to bargain. All we do is take our helpless, sinful, little selves and fling them on God's mercy. God is waiting.

The wonder of all this is that God does not do this by a command but by getting down into intimate relationships with us. When there is a restored relationship, when we know God to be living in our souls, we cannot continue to be the same persons committing the same old sins.

Our inevitable reaction is one of gratitude. The Christian cannot try to manufacture this attitude. What we can do is try to meet Christ at such a level that gratitude will spontaneously flow. Gratitude is simply a description of the meeting, of what happens when a human soul meets God at this level. The most profound thing possible has occurred. We have been released from the spiral, from a fate worse than death. We know that we have been transferred from a kingdom of darkness to a kingdom of light. We who were dead in sins are now alive in Christ. We do not have to create fellowship or belonging; we simply belong to a common deliverer. Christ has done this. We are in the fellowship of the delivered, the reconciled, the justified, the freed, the forgiven.

We naturally keep pointing to the One who has brought this deliverance. Sometimes people grow weary of hearing us talk about it, but we can't keep quiet. We must be witnesses to Jesus Christ. This, the church, has grown out of the experience of reconciliation and forgiveness. We belong, not because we initiate the belonging, but because we have entered into the experience which has been provided by Christ.

> There is a green hill far away with out a city wall,
> Where the dear Lord was crucified; who died to save us all,
> We may not know, we cannot tell, what pains he had to
>   bear,
> But we know that it was for us, he hung and suffered there.
> There was none other good enough to pay the price of sin,
> He only could unlock the gate of heaven, and let us in.[1]

Note

[1] Hymn No. 171, "There Is a Green Hill Far Away," lyrics by Cecil F. Alexander, *Pilgrim Hymnal* (New York: Pilgrim Press, 1980).

15

Reducing Fear

~

This 1989 homily offers encouragement to those who struggle with the restraints of fear. During this period several major missions faced severe challenges.

All of the chapters of Scripture are amazing, but the eighth chapter of Matthew is especially amazing. Jesus has completed what we call the Sermon on the Mount (as compiled by Matthew), and immediately afterward has come down from the mountain. Matthew writes:

> After he had come down from the hill he was followed by a great crowd. And now a leper approached him, bowed low, and said, "Sir, if only you will, you can cleanse me." Jesus stretched out his hand, touched him, and said, "Indeed I will; be clean again." And his leprosy was cured immediately. . . .
> When he had entered into Capernaum a centurion came up to ask his help. "Sir," he said, "a boy of mine lies at home paralysed and racked with pain." Jesus said, "I will come and cure him." (8:1–7)

We never find any reluctance in Jesus. He is always ready to come. "He loves to say yes," as Carolyn Parr has put it in one of the songs she has written.

> But the centurion replied, "Sir, who am I to have you under my roof? You need only say the word and the boy will be cured. I know, for I am myself under orders, with soldiers under me. I say to one, 'Go,' and he goes; to another, 'Come here,' and he comes; and to my servant, 'Do this,' and he does it." Jesus heard him with astonishment, and said to the people who were following him, "I tell you this: nowhere, even in Israel, have I

found such faith." . . . Then Jesus said to the centurion, "Go home now; because of your faith, so let it be." At that moment the boy recovered.

Jesus then went to Peter's house and found Peter's mother-in-law in bed with fever. So he took her by the hand; the fever left her; and she got up and waited on him.

When evening fell, they brought to him many who were possessed by devils; and he drove the spirits out with a word and healed all who were sick, to fulfill the prophecy of Isaiah: "He took away our illnesses and lifted our diseases from us."

At the sight of the crowds surrounding him Jesus gave word to cross to the other shore. A doctor of the law came up, and said, "Master, I will follow you wherever you go." Jesus replied, "Foxes have their holes, the birds their roosts; but the Son of Man has nowhere to lay his head." Another man, one of his disciples, said to him, "Lord, let me go and bury my father first." Jesus replied, "Follow me, and leave the dead to bury their dead."

Jesus then got into the boat, and his disciples followed. All at once a great storm arose on the lake, till the waves were breaking right over the boat; but he went on sleeping. So they came and woke him up, crying: "Save us, Lord; we are sinking!" [You don't seem to be aware of what's going on. We're going down!]

"Why are you such cowards?" he said; "how little faith you have!" Then he stood up and rebuked the wind and the sea, and there was a dead calm. The men were astonished at what had happened, and exclaimed, "What sort of man is this? Even the wind and the sea obey him!"

When he reached the other side, in the country of the Gadarenes, he was met by two men who came out from the tombs; they were possessed by devils, and so violent that no one dared pass that way. "You son of God," they shouted, "what do you want with us? Have you come here to torment us before our time?" In the distance a large herd of pigs was feeding; and the devils begged him: "If you drive us out, send us into that herd of pigs." "Begone!" he said. Then they came out and went into the pigs; the whole herd rushed over the edge into the lake, and perished in the water.

The men in charge of them took to their heels, and made for the town, where they told the whole story, and what had happened to the madmen. Thereupon all the town came out to meet Jesus; and when they saw him they begged him to leave the district and go. [We'd like to get these mentally ill people feeling better, but we don't want you around. This is not the right neighborhood.] (Matt. 8:8–34)

All this is found in the eighth chapter of Matthew. One day you may want to read it, ponder it, and appropriate it for yourself. You would find it a profitable experience.

We are all living in some degree of fear. How do we reduce the level of our fear? In the Scriptures faith and fear are closely related. A deeper level of faith reduces the level of fear. We are commanded to have faith. "Believe in God," said Jesus; "believe also in me" [Have faith in me.] (John 14:1, *RSV*).

We are commanded to give up fear. The first words spoken by an angel in the announcement of news or by Jesus as he greets a friend are often, "Fear not."

Faith and fear are central components of life. Life can be paralyzed by fear. On the other hand, life can be expanded and enhanced immeasurably by faith.

Because they are central to life, fear and faith are central to the New Testament since the Scriptures are concerned primarily with life's enhancement. "I came that they may have life, and have it abundantly"(John 10:10, *RSV*). As someone has said, "If you refuse to give up fear, you don't believe the New Testament." Fear restricts life, paralyzes it. To live in fear is to live a miserably restricted life.

Although we may not have examined this aspect of our lives, it is undeniable that each of us lives at a certain level of fear: a high level, a medium level, sometimes at a minimal level. And our level of fear affects almost everything we do or fail to do.

I believe we have a degree of control over our fear level—over whether that fear is reduced or essentially eliminated during a period of time. There are times when we cannot control our fear, and at those times, we need to be pastorally sensitive to one another. To rebuke another when he or she is near panic is not especially helpful. We do that quite frequently when we say, "You shouldn't feel that way."

On the other hand (and everything has its "on the other hand"), Jesus rebuked the disciples in the midst of their fear and panic. He was preparing them for times which would be much more difficult. He knew that their fear level could be reduced. And his genuine love could pinpoint the problem for them.

The problem was faith. Faith could be deepened. Jesus knew it. God could be trusted, because God is trustworthy and faithful. He, Jesus, could be trusted. Why be fearful, and thus have life restricted and paralyzed, when there is an ultimate safety in the universe, and nothing—absolutely nothing—to fear? If Jesus is king of the flood, why fear the flood?

When Jesus rebuked the disciples during the storm, he was concerned because their fear meant that they had missed his central message. The central message that he had been incarnating was that the Father/Mother God was loving and could be trusted in every circumstance.

The fact that they were panicked in the storm meant that although they had accepted the truth conceptually—had spiritualized it—they had not absorbed it inwardly where their life was affected. They were restricted by their fear. Jesus had called them to do audacious things— things that were totally impossible for them to do as long as their fear level was so high.

The assumption of the Bible is that fear can not only be transcended but, for all practical purposes, can be eliminated. I John 4:18 says, "Perfect love casts out fear" *(RSV)*—not just most of it but all of it.

You have all met people who believe and will tell you that they have an anxious, fearful temperament and must just live with it as gracefully as possible. Thus, they suffer more than others, and they want you to know it. They say, "Better to accept that reality than to fight it." This unfortunate attitude seems to excuse them from the rigors of the inner faith journey.

God is trustworthy, and we can learn to trust deeply that reality. Fearful people can become fearless people. The cringing, fearful, panicked disciples at Golgotha became fearless, brave, courageous, towering figures, who left provincial Galilee and established faith communities in many places in their then-known world. Fully willing to die if necessary, some of them became the martyrs of the church.

Experiencing the resurrection always means the release of new, mysterious, divine powers which inevitably affect the fear level of the person involved. Every mortal power, including the power of death, is ultimately experienced as impotent in the presence of the newly released resurrection power. In this new light all the mortal powers, experienced before as formidable and frightening in their swaggering pretensions, are perceived to be innocuous—even ridiculous. As the Psalmist says of the people who think they have power: "He who sits in the heavens laughs; the LORD has them in derision" (Ps. 2:4, *RSV*).

Let us be very clear that faith is not simply a general feeling of confidence—not a good feeling about oneself, not just a strong self-image, though sometimes these are good attitudes to have.

In the biblical sense, in the Christian sense, faith is an awareness of an attachment, a belonging to a Person, the person of the resurrected Christ, who has invaded us in response to our longing and openness. This One will never for a moment leave us. "I will never fail you nor forsake you" (Hebrews 13:5, *RSV*). He will never leave us orphaned. He has linked his eternal destiny with ours; in him we are safe and secure forever, whatever life's vicissitudes may be.

Faith is faith in Jesus Christ and his eternal love for us; faith in his future, and our linkage with that future. I am linked with the future of Jesus Christ, and he seems to be getting along pretty well, roaming around the universe in his cosmic, resurrected presence, looking forward to the culmination, the Shalom. I am linked with that future because he has made a covenant with me forever.

Faith in the deepening love of that Person really reduces fear—even has the possibility of eliminating fear. In his presence all the worldly powers are simply defeated, kaput, overcome. They can be treated with a kind of respect because they put up such a fight, and it took us so long to see them for what they are. They were cunningly deceitful. But now we can laugh at them, because Christ has treated them like a discarded garment. They are impotent. They are ridiculous. "We are more than conquerors through him who loved us" (Rom. 8:37, *RSV*).

Have you ever seriously reflected on how different your life might be now—how many decisions might have been made differently in the past—if your fear level had been lower?

Suppose that your present fear level were reduced by 50 percent. What could you imagine yourself doing? Some of us could scarcely wait to start doing all we have secretly wished to do—being all we have wished to be. And that would be our feeling if our fear level were reduced by just 50 percent. What would our reaction be if our fear level were totally eliminated? So often the fear that held us in check and kept us ordinary and mediocre has kept us from statesmanlike servant leadership.

Matthew's Gospel, chapter 8, describes three stages in the spiritual life, each of which is affected in a major way by the fear level, as are all the phases of our lives today and all the decisions that we make. Fritz Kunkel in *Creation Continues* describes the movement and interprets the psychology of this chapter in a very helpful way, for which I feel indebted to him[1]:

The first and determinative phase of the reducing of the fear level is that of deciding seriously and decisively to respond to Christ's call to follow him. His call to each person—woman, man, child—is very simple: "Follow me. Follow me. Follow me." Two words: "Follow me."

Now the hearing of that call usually comes after "hanging around" Jesus and Jesus' crowd for a period of time. Whenever you go to a church which is an authentic church, you are hanging around Jesus, because Jesus is the cohering power which holds that community together. And all of the people in an authentic church are the crowd hanging around Jesus.

You will not find concentration on Jesus in some churches. And sometimes you will have to look carefully to find it in this one. Last week in a class in Christian Doctrine I asked a question: "Why is it that it's so difficult for us to talk about Jesus naturally? We can talk about mission, talk about the inner life, about the outward journey, about structures, about the poor. But it is very hard for people who are reasonably sophisticated to talk about Jesus. Yet, we're the crowd hanging around Jesus."

The call usually comes after hanging around Jesus, perceiving the magnetism of his person, and being attracted by him. We may see a few things such as miracles or manifestations of transcendence that are not too easily explained.

Miraculous happenings are exactly what Matthew records—things that happened to people who were just hanging around. We have tried to make it easy through the years for people just to hang around The Church of the Saviour—not to do anything—not even usher, not sing in the choir, not do anything at all. People ought to be comfortable hanging around, not being asked to do anything. But then there is the flip side, and somehow there is always a flip side. People may feel that such a hands-off attitude on our part is an indication of indifference. They think, "I can hang around forever, and they may never ask me to do anything."

The people who were hanging around Jesus saw several things in one day's time: They saw a leper healed. That was an amazing thing. A centurion's boy, paralyzed and racked with pain, was healed. They saw a woman, Peter's mother-in-law, in bed with a high fever. Jesus took her by the hand; she recovered and prepared a meal for him.

Many possessed by devils came and were healed. All of these things they saw—those people who were just hanging around. Amazing!

The time came, however, for Jesus to move on. He gave word to cross over to the other side. In a moment he would be getting into the boat. And those seriously following him must get into the boat where the teaching would continue for them. The others would go back home and promptly forget it all, as most people in the afternoon forget the sermon they hear in the morning.

Those in the boat would be in close and intimate contact with Jesus. There they would get to know him. They would share the storms of his life with him. They would engage in mission with him. They would tackle demented, violent men inhabited by devils. Either they got into the boat or they were left behind with their wistfulness and memories.

According to Kunkel, there were two classes represented here. One was a doctor of the law, a seminary graduate, well educated. With all his credentials, recognizing the mediocrity and meaningless of his life contrasted with the new reality that he was experiencing by hanging around, he said to Jesus, "You're going to get into the boat. I want to go with you. I will follow you wherever you go."

Jesus' response is very interesting. He said, "I, unlike you, Sir, have no established place in the world of the influential and powerful. If you take tonight's boat ride with me, you go into a world where your credentials mean nothing. You go with me, knowing that I am an unsheltered person. 'Foxes have holes and birds have their nests.' I want you to come, but I must be totally honest with you. I want you to understand the situation."

Another man, perhaps representing the peasant class, with a strong loyalty to the traditional values, also wanted to go. His problem was different. He had no place of status or privilege to leave, no credentials. He was not concerned about that kind of security. His loyalty was to the traditional family values and ties.

He said to Jesus, "Listen, Jesus. I've really been excited hanging around here today. My family will not understand though, if I engage in this precipitate, erratic behavior. If I take the boat out tonight, they will never get over it. They'll try to understand. They will say, 'Yes, he's done this sort of thing before.' But they will never understand. So I will stay, Jesus, and look after things until the old man dies, and we settle the estate. Then I'll be free from these responsibilities. I understand that you'll probably be in Capernaum, and I'll look you up and really follow you then."

Jesus replied, "My dear friend, this is the moment. You've seen it. You've sensed who I am. You've seen the manifestations of the new kingdom. The boat won't be back. Those who haven't glimpsed the new will carry on their old life. Follow me now, tonight. This boat, this moment won't return. Everything that you have seen today will fade into a swamp of memories and regrets. This boat won't be back. You won't find me in Capernaum later. I'm going to a cross in Jerusalem."

Now the question is, did either of these two men go? We are not told. Whichever way the decision went, surely fear had a lot to do with it: fear of a life cut loose from the old securities, fear of disapproval of family, fear of the new—new frontiers, new tasks, new relationships. You make the list. It goes on and on.

But let us suppose they made the decision to follow, drawn by the person of Jesus, sensing his divinity, sensing the excitement of a divine kingdom breaking into the present moment. Let us assume that they got into the boat with him. Then we move into the second phase.

The next stage is one of turbulence—storm. Breaking from the old, launching out into the new, always means inner turbulence and outer turbulence. Anybody who tells you that if you get into the boat with Jesus everything is going to work out well forever after just doesn't understand the faith. The next stage is turbulence.

Inner questions. Wonderings. Can you imagine the inner questions felt that stormy night by that Ph.D.? And by the peasant, leaving his life and the traditional family values?

I suspect that at times one of them wished that he'd gone back south, by land, to be with the rabbis in the rabbinical school in Jerusalem. A storm is brewing, and he's in this boat! And this is something he's never done before! You can just imagine how upset he is! He says, "Those guys are going to be talking about all these issues tomorrow morning, and I'm going to miss out on all the theological discussions. And I don't even know whether this boat's going to get to shore tonight! This is the most stupid thing I have ever done in my life!"

Once the peasant began to think about having followed his impulse, I suspect that he regretted flouting the family values. And he wished that he could be home with Daddy.

Something happened that night. The storm ceased. There was a dead calm. The elements were quieted, and there was an inner, living calm. A hush. And they exclaimed, "What sort of man is this? Even the wind and the sea obey him!" They knew him in a new way that night, and knowing him in the intimacy of the boat, in the storm, they were never as fearful again. They were fearful, but they were never as fearful again. Their fear level had been reduced.

There's a third phase. Rather than giving his disciples a sabbatical following the terrible storm, he landed with them in Gadarene territory and immediately took them into the presence of the demonic.

He was met by two men who came out from the tombs. They were possessed by devils, and so violent that "no one dared pass that way." Jesus always goes into the presence of the demonic. And he takes his disciples with him.

Imagine the fear of the disciples: "Listen, Jesus, everybody's talking about this. This is no place to be. Let's skirt the area and this problem, as everybody else does. We can bypass it." Can you imagine the poor Ph.D? He hadn't ever had this sort of experience. This was quite different from being an observer in the midst of the crowd before he got into the boat. Here his credentials are totally worthless. Those demoniacs don't care a thing in the world about his degrees.

Here he knows he's identified as a follower of the leader. What happens to Jesus happens to him. It was that way when all the miracles were taking place. But this is an entirely different situation— much tougher. He knows that he cannot slip away from the crowd now. He becomes a victim. Whatever happens to Jesus happens to him.

Quite an assignment for one who hasn't even completed the courses in the School of Christian Living! Here he is—out here with the demoniacs! After being with Jesus only one night. One night!!

The homeless, mentally ill were healed, but this incident upset the economic arrangements of the region. The economic costs were too high, and Jesus and his little band were asked to leave. They, the people in the region, preferred to have things as they were, status quo.

Jesus always takes us into the midst of the demonic, and he reduces our fear sufficiently to enable us to name it as evil, to look it squarely in the face. For people not to have housing is evil. Every one of us should be furious that there is no adequate housing policy for low-income people. We are not doing anything about it yet. The debate is on, but nothing is happening. That is evil.

For children to be raised by children and not trained for work in our society is evil. For the mentally ill to be treated as they were treated a hundred years ago, and worse, is evil. For the homeless sick to have legs amputated for lack of medical attention—and every one of us who has been to Christ House has seen those examples—that is evil.

To spend our world resources for armaments and bombs and weapons, to take from the environment what we are taking, and to take from the poor what we are taking are evils. There is no way to state it except just that way. We do not even have to use the weapons to destroy the planet. Just the fact that we are making them destroys the planet. We are killing ourselves by making them. It is a sin to make them.

We can go into the midst of the Gadarene territory and, in and through Jesus, heal a few demoniacs. But often we are told to leave. One of the easiest ways for people to tell us to leave is simply not to support us. If we are in there and we have no money, they use that reason to tell us to leave.

The society is saying, "Don't shake up our economic arrangements. We like it the way it is for the privileged few. And we're perfectly willing to take it from the ones who are least able to afford it. Please leave us alone! Don't even remind us. You're sending us too many letters describing what's going on, saying that you need our help."

Whether we can look it all squarely in the eye depends upon our fear level. Many hate the poor, because they fear the poor. Our society hates criminals. We hate the mentally ill, because we fear them. We fear and hate, yet we claim to follow Jesus, who commands us to give up fear and love literally everybody, especially our enemies. This inner schism is very serious and cries out for healing. If this schism is not healed, we are not saved. Forgiveness of our sins means we have the capacity to love everybody for Jesus' sake and are willing to die out of that love if and when to die is necessary.

Through the Scripture—and through the Scripture through me today—Jesus is calling you now to *follow him*. That needs to be a clear decision. Not just, "I'm hanging around"; but, "No matter what happens and no matter how frightened I am, I commit myself today to belong to Jesus forever. Jesus, I declare, is Lord of my life—Jesus, the person of Jesus."

I would call you to that first step. Make it very, very clear.

The second step is to begin the night sea journey through the storms.

If you get into the boat, he will never leave you. The question is whether you will get into the boat. If you will get into the boat, he will never leave you alone.

Despite being taken by Jesus into the Gadarene territory, into the presence of the demonic, you'll be so drawn by the power of a great affection that your fear will slip away. "In the world you will have trouble. But courage! The victory is mine; I have conquered the world" (John 16:33).

And, "Peace is my parting gift to you, my own peace, such as the world cannot give. Set your troubled hearts at rest, and banish your fears" (John 14:27).

Note

[1] Fritz Kunkel, *Creation Continues: A Psychological Interpretation of the First Gospel* (New York: C. Scribner's Sons, 1947).

16

Detachment

~

By 1988 many missions that had been started by The Church of the Saviour had become much larger than the resources of the small church were able to maintain. In the face of these challenges Gordon advocated a broader perspective.

Let us consider several Scriptures. The first is from Hebrews:

> Then indeed his voice shook the earth, but now he has prom-
> ised, "Yet once again I will shake not earth alone, but the
> heavens also." The words "once again"—and only once—imply
> that the shaking of these created things means their removal,
> and then what is not shaken will remain. The kingdom we are
> given is unshakable; let us therefore give thanks to God, and so
> worship him as he would be worshipped, with reverence and
> awe; for our God is a devouring fire. (12:26–29)

From 2 Corinthians:

> No wonder we do not lose heart! [When Paul starts a passage
> with those words, written in the midst of the arduous times in
> which the apostles were living—and while I know what our own
> people are facing in these days—I want to find out why he says
> they do not lose heart.] Though our outward humanity is in
> decay, yet day by day we are inwardly renewed. Our troubles
> are slight and short-lived; and their outcome an eternal glory
> which outweighs them far. Meanwhile our eyes are fixed, not on
> the things that are seen, but on the things that are unseen; for
> what is seen passes away; what is unseen is eternal. For we
> know that if the earthly frame that houses us today should be
> demolished, we possess a building which God has provided—a

house not made by human hands, eternal, and in heaven. In this present body we do indeed groan; we yearn to have our heavenly habitation put on over this one—in the hope that, being thus clothed, we shall not find ourselves naked. We groan indeed, we who are enclosed within this earthly frame; we are oppressed because we do not want to have the old body stripped off. Rather our desire is to have the new body put on over it, so that our mortal part may be absorbed into life immortal. God himself has shaped us for this very end; and as a pledge of it he has given us the Spirit.

Therefore we never cease to be confident. We know that so long as we are at home in the body we are exiles from the Lord; faith is our guide, we do not see him. We are confident, I repeat, and would rather leave our home in the body and go to live with the Lord. We therefore make it our ambition, wherever we are, here or there, to be acceptable to him. For we must all have our lives laid open before the tribunal of Christ [and that is a threat or a promise of blessing, whichever way you want to look at it], where each must receive what is due to him for his conduct in the body, good or bad. (4:16—5:1-10)

Fundamental to being a Christian is becoming a contemplative. In an unpublished part of Thomas Merton's writing he talks about how difficult it is to become a contemplative, even in a monastery. Then he says:

But at the other extreme, we have the isolated lay person, trying to keep up an interior life in the world, without the support of any institutional structure and without any defense against the pressures and distractions of secular life.

Now, if it is hard to prepare for contemplative life even in a monastery, how much harder will it be outside one? It can be truly said that for very many people, for this reason, the contemplative life is simply out of the question. . . .

Even for those best endowed and prepared, the ordinary conditions of urban life today are so inimical to spirituality that they will have to keep up a ceaseless struggle if they are to enjoy even the most elementary kind of interior life.

After talking about how difficult and seemingly impossible it is to live this kind of life, Merton continues:

It seems right to say that one who wants a contemplative life today, whether in a monastery or in the world, must do two things:

> First, he must, as far as possible, reduce the conflict and frustration in his life by cutting down his contact with the world and his secular subjections. This means reducing his needs for pleasure, comfort, recreation, prestige, and success, and embracing a life of true spiritual poverty and detachment.
>
> Secondly, this person must learn to put up with the inevitable conflicts that remain—the noise, the agitation, the crowding, the lack of time, and above all, the constant contact with the purely secular mentality which is all around us everywhere and at all times, even to some extent in monasteries.

Let us consider the first condition, that of embracing a life of true spiritual poverty and detachment, which reduces our contact with the world.

What Merton is saying, we all know. Everyone today is living under pressure. This is a pressure era in our world's history, and probably greater than ever before, because everybody knows everything; we are all in touch with what is going on all over the world. And we have the instruments to make people's lives miserable on a cosmic scale.

The world is in turmoil. The anxiety level throughout the world is very high, often near panic. Sometimes it moves over the panic level, and people operate out of their panic.

In our deeps we all know this. The world is playing Russian roulette, and the chamber fired next may be the end of everything. Though we try to deaden the fear, no drug is adequate.

In addition, many of us have taken on the pain of the oppressed—oppressed and abused children, the mentally ill, the elderly, the homeless, the poor. This is another level of pressure for those who are sensitized and are struggling valiantly against "Pharaoh," or the dominant consciousness. These persons are being persecuted, pressured in a variety of ways for Christ's sake and his kingdom. There is the general pressure of the times, and there is the special pressure for those of us who have consciously entered the fray against evil.

The toll for many of us is extremely heavy, and some find that they cannot take it. Others remain borderline for many years. They have difficulty sleeping and exhibit psychosomatic symptoms of various kinds. They go around tired and heavy most of the time, near burnout, but determined to be faithful to the end.

We are burdened by a feeling of "oughtness," and we attempt to hold on. Consciousness comes at a very high price—but the price is much higher for unconsciousness.

The question, then, is this: Is there any real relief from the pressure that often threatens to do us in? Can we be detached from events and people in circumstances that threaten to overwhelm us?

We are commanded to do two things, which seem to be in conflict with each other. We are commanded to become detached. We are also commanded to become attached more deeply to the world's pain. Is attachment at ever-deeper levels possible at the same time that we become detached? Is there any balm in Gilead for our spirits? Jesus says, "I give you my peace, the peace which passes all understanding." But is peace really possible if we are connected, if we are conscious, if we have taken on the pain of the world?

Scripture affirms that there are different levels of reality—the surface level and the deeper level. The deeper level—the one of perfect peace, wonder, surprise—is available every moment. It can be reached now. No need to wait until later to plumb its depths.

The surface level is always there, swirling with events, circumstances, problems, worries. On this surface level one is sick, feeling bad; the body is dying and the tasks confronting us are impossible and overwhelming.

In the deeps, the level which the Scripture says is the unseen level, something else takes place. Here there is perfect health. The body is not dying; the resurrection body is forming. In the deeps there is no confusion, no complexity—only the present moment and the one thing we are to see and revel in and, in that moment, do.

The surface is always obviously, painfully there, but the deeps are also always there. By selectively remembering and driving the stakes of our lives down into those deeps, we can know a detachment from the swirling events on the surface. Learning to withdraw energy from the surface, we focus energy in the deeps.

These two levels are clearly set forth in Scripture. On one level we live in the kingdom of God; on the other level we live on the surface in the kingdoms of this world. In the deeps we are not living on the visible surface primarily. We are withdrawing energy from, and, in a sense, forgetting the surface, remembering the deeps.

In this way we come to be rooted in transcendence, the transcendence of the moment. In that moment there is no need to know anything. There is no need, in that moment, to do anything. There is no need, in that moment, to possess anything. We require no minimum comfort level; we insist on no minimum support from others. Every surface thing can be forgotten in the remembering of the deep. We are simply touching an infinite realm of grace and compassion in the presence of the Father/Mother God. In that moment we know a forgiving relationship. The enmity is broken, and we know a gloriously consummated future, unsurpassed in its splendor.

Although easy to describe, actually to live in such a moment of transcendence is very, very difficult. We need to be aware of the difficulties. We must remember that, if we are highly conscious and if we are interconnected with other people, every moment presents problems for which there are no answers, demands which seem conflicting, and even bad feelings directed toward us.

Growing closer to the kingdom does not mean that we are further away from people who have bad feelings about us. If that were so, Jesus would not have encountered people with bad feelings toward him. He lived in the midst of people who harbored bad feelings, and those people finally killed him.

Certain moments will bring the pressures of people who have bad feelings toward us. Other moments will bring fundamental uncertainties concerning the future, suffering and, for many of us, imminent death. Each such moment is really a microcosm of the old order, which is at odds with the new order; and each, in itself, is always a mixed moment. Most often discouraging, always messy, never neat, every moment comes with countless, hanging, loose threads. We think we have something all wrapped up—but we never have anything wrapped up. Nothing is ever in place. It may seem to be in place just because mentally we have wrapped up a few things and have said it is in place. But that is a mental way of making ourselves feel comfortable. None of the loose ends of our lives is ever wrapped up.

Our own characters are always strange mixtures of divinity and pathology. Some facets of our lives are working well; others hang on the brink of destruction. And all of these things are taking place in the same moment.

The world may make it; it may not make it. We don't know. We may rape the environment until it turns on us and is no longer willing or able to sustain us.

The hard-to-face reality is that this mixture will be the content of every succeeding moment for the rest of our lives. Such is the nature of the continuum in which we live. The nature of the given moment is much more cruel for some than for others. We must try to relieve the pain of those who are caught in the crueler circumstances. But every future moment for every one of us will consist of this ambiguous mixture. We are always hoping that things will quiet down in the future. They never will.

The question is whether, in this moment, this surface-forgetting can occur and transcendence and deep celebration will take place.

The old saints speak of the sacrament of the present moment—the prime importance of living into the Now. But we tend to keep putting it off. "Another time" we will learn to live in the deeps in the present moment. "Later," we say, "it will happen." The later time comes, and it fails to happen. Old age arrives, and the time for dying occurs. The Now, delayed, has never been lived.

To return to the question: Is it possible, in the midst of this kind of world—messy and filled with all the problems that we know about—to live in the deeps? Or are there some circumstances which make it just too difficult?

The answer is that no circumstances are too difficult. Scripture teaches that, even in the most difficult circumstances, when we touch those depths we can withdraw energy from a world which is entirely different from the world of the surface.

Just a few hours before his execution, Jesus is with his disciples. He knows they are going to forsake him and flee. And what is he doing? He is saying to the Father, "I feel your presence with me. I am not alone. And I pray for these men. I thank you, God, for the wonderful gift they have been to me." [They've been a wonderful mission group.] Every one of them is going to betray him or forsake him. But he says, "I am not alone," because even at that crucial time he is living in those depths.

A little later, in the beginning of his ordeal on the cross, because of his identification with all of us in our brokenness and our woundedness, he was unable to sense God's presence. But toward the end of the ordeal he came to know that presence, and he was able to say, "Father, into your hands I commend my spirit." Even though he did not understand what was happening, he sensed God's being. He was living in those depths.

Stephen? Being stoned to death, he saw an opening in the sky. He saw Jesus. He was in that presence in the deeps of his own being even while he was being stoned.

We cannot argue, "My circumstances are insurmountable." I can know and draw energy from the deeps regardless of circumstances.

We need to prepare; we need to struggle; we need to work with this concept. Matthew Fox suggests two important principles. The first principle is that of "letting be." The second is "letting go."

One of the most crucial dimensions of letting be is the recognition that there is no need to change the event or the person. The ability to let be is extremely rare and demands a respect and reverence beyond most of us. We argue, "Shouldn't we want to change the undesirable event, to change the person who obviously needs changing?" I believe the answer is no.

We can be there, knowing that God's presence can be there in us and through us and that whatever changes are appropriate will occur. That attitude is quite different from a feeling that we must struggle to change people and try to change events. There is very little celebration, transcendence, and lifting of the burdens of others when we are hoping to change them and clean them up. Through the years I have found that the attempt to get another cleaned up can be a very heavy burden. And to try to get a community cleaned up is an even heavier burden.

The task is to enjoy the other, to experience the wonder of the person more, to be more open, to be more attentive, to learn more from the person or the community, and to revel in the surprises given. If the person or the community changes—good. If not, we have celebrated, lived in the Now.

If you feel you can't tolerate the mess, the only advice I can give to you is: choose what for you is a better mess, if you can find it. But wherever you go, you go to the next mess. You may take a couple of years to find out how messy it is. But you will find it to be a mess.

We need to remember that the Father/Mother God not only tolerates but delights in the present moment of being of all of us who by faith are in God—and God has tolerated many messes for many eons.

To insist on changing the person or the event makes it impossible to let be and to celebrate, to live in the Now, to live in the depths.

To let be and let go is to have no need to know what is going to happen—how things are going to turn out. When one lives in the depths, one simply prefers to be open to the surprises of the moment and of all future moments, rather than to know the outcome.

Moreover, there is no need to do. Of course, I will do many things, but with no compulsive need to do, no quota of work. No achievements must be completed within an allotted time span. Instead, my doing will grow out of this moment of being, of play, of re-creation, of celebration.

There is also no need to possess anything, to cling, to control. Anything needed will be given in the next moment. It will appear as surprise; there is no need to clutch. The sole rule of the present moment and the ability to live in, and celebrate it constitute the deepest appropriation of our faith in God's grace through our Lord, Jesus Christ.

All of this involves, of course, the recognition of our finiteness, our creatureliness, our having so many things that we cannot do anything about. But because we are made in God's image and are co-creators with God, we can become makers of history; we can change the direction of the lives of thousands of people. None of us has ever reached the limit of what we can be and do. That is one side of it. And we forget that to our peril.

When we consider the flip side of this maker-of-history role in which all of us are cast, we must admit we cannot do anything about a good many things—things that wait on the freedom of the other. We have reached our limits, and even God waits and cannot do anything. So the awareness of our creaturely limits is absolutely essential. We just cannot fix things that we would like to fix.

Detachment is the capacity to treat the surface level very lightly. Because one is rooted in the eternal Now that is beneath the surface, one experiences a deeper mystery which is unshakable. The Hebrew Scripture says that all that can be shaken will be removed; only the deeps will not be shaken and cannot be removed. One is being washed, bathed in grace.

In detachment, one ceases hanging on to all that is worrisome: thousands of petty details about the children, about dying parents, about our own imminent death if we have been pronounced incurably sick. At one level such concerns need attention. You will attend to them when it becomes necessary. But you will drop all of those things that nag at you, weigh you down. You just do not take them on. You can care deeply about things that you do not take on. Detachment, sitting loose from the surface, is possible when you are deeply rooted in that reality which will never pass away.

This journey into the deeps is extremely costly. But it is the one journey which is worth reflecting on every waking moment and dreaming about whenever we sleep.

And so I would ask that we pray for journeying mercies for one another as we begin our pilgrimage at a new level.

Part VI

~·~

Expanding Vision, Reaching Out

17

Deepening Connections

~

In 1990 Gordon continued to affirm a faith that God is, and will be, with us. We are not alone and the vitality of the divine presence is ours for the asking.

In an amazing passage in the eighth chapter of Romans beginning with the eighteenth verse, Paul writes, "I reckon that the sufferings we now endure bear no comparison with the splendor, as yet unrevealed, which is in store for us."

Having tried to take that in, we read further:

> The created universe waits with eager expectation for God's sons [and daughters] to be revealed. It was made the victim of frustration, not by its own choice, but because of him who made it so; yet always there was hope, because the universe itself is to be freed from the shackles of mortality and enter upon the liberty and splendour of the children of God. Up to the present, we know [and Paul was writing two thousand years ago, before the whole created universe got into the trouble that it is in now], the whole created universe groans in all its parts as if in the pangs of childbirth." (Rom. 8:18–22)

In the beginning of *The Coming of the Cosmic Christ*, Matthew Fox says that Albert Einstein was once asked, "What is the most important question you can ask in life?" Einstein answered, "Is the universe a friendly place or not?"[1]

Evelyn Underhill put the same question another way: "Is the universe safe for souls?" That is, is it the place where souls can unfold?

Fox goes on to say:

In the first century of this era when Jesus lived in Palestine, and during the time when the Gospel stories about him were being written, the most important question in the Mediterranean civilization was, "Are the angels friend or foe?" Since angels were understood to be the driving force behind the elements of the universe, it is clear that, like Einstein, the people of that era wanted to know whether or not the universe was a friendly place.

To that same question the early Christians had a definite response: Jesus represented the smiling face of God.[2]

Jesus said that the universe was friendly for us. All of the demonic powers, including the invisible angels, were ultimately overcome in the life, death, and resurrection of Jesus.

We immediately sense the importance of the question. Unless we believe the universe to be friendly in all of its various manifestations, we surely will not relax into it. We will not seek to deepen our connections with it. To connect deeply is to relax into, to give to, to receive from, to trust, to let down, to be cared for, to be nourished by, to nourish.

When we question the friendliness of the universe, we take a stance of resistance, defensiveness. We naturally seek to protect ourselves from it. We erect defenses against it. We seek to exist as isolated individuals protecting our precarious, isolated existence. We become cut off and lonely. And often, in that state of "cut-off-ness," we become very angry or we become deeply depressed. (Many people are very angry, angry at life or at something I or someone else said.)

Alice Miller, the psychiatrist, tells us that depression is the result of being separated from one's true self. The stance of defensiveness contradicts our deep nature. We are made to trust, to be nurtured, to connect with the whole, to be persons deeply attuned to the whole universe in which we live. But the protective stance makes us fugitives from all that we were intended to be and to be at home with.

We can look upon the universe as friendly, as a hostile universe, or as a neutral universe. However it affects us, it impinges upon us primarily in three ways.

First, God comes to us directly. Second, God and the universe impinge upon us through people. We would like, many of us, to separate God from people, because God somehow feels more friendly than people. But God comes to us through people, and people are a part of the universe. Third, God comes to us through the whole creation, through the created order. All three are ways of connecting with God. These ways are not really separated, as we often feel them to be. All of them have to do with our redemption through Jesus Christ. Let us look at these three areas.

God comes to us directly. We experience God with the mystic dimension of our natures. A function of the right lobe of the brain, this dimension of our natures is, for most of us, seriously undeveloped.

One woman, after attending a workshop having to do with the understanding of these different dimensions, went home and had a dream. She dreamed that the left lobe of her brain was gigantic, like a skyscraper with many stories. The right lobe of her brain was like a dried-up prune.

This very good image depicts how developed we are in one area, and how very undeveloped in another area. For three hundred years, especially since the Enlightenment, we have worked much more with the left brain than with the right.

The left lobe is generally recognized as controlling functions of analysis and verbalization, while the right lobe is primarily responsible for synthesis, for connection-making, for experiencing of the whole.

Mystical ability is psychologically located in the right lobe of the brain. And as we develop the mystical dimension of our being, we can experience God directly. God comes to us and speaks to us directly. All of us have had such an experience at one time or another.

Matthew Fox tells that Martin Luther King, Jr., had an experience of this mystical directness about two weeks after he had organized the bus boycott in Montgomery, Alabama.

> [King] was receiving phone calls threatening him and his family daily. Finally he received a call at midnight that said, "If you aren't out of town in three days we're going to blow your brains out and blow up your house."
>
> King comments: "I sat there and thought about a beautiful little daughter who had just been born. . . . I started thinking about a dedicated, devoted, and loyal wife, who was over there asleep. . . . And I discovered that religion had to become real to me, and I had to know God for myself.
>
> "And I bowed down over that cup of coffee. I never will forget it. . . . I prayed a prayer, and I prayed out loud that night. . . . 'I'm faltering. I'm losing my courage. And I can't let the people see me like this because if they see me weak and losing my courage, they will begin to get weak.' . . . And it seemed at that

moment that I could hear an inner voice saying to me, 'Martin
Luther, stand up for righteousness. Stand up for justice. Stand
up for truth. And lo, I will be with you, even until the end of the
world.' He promised never to leave me, never to leave me
alone. No never alone."[3]

A direct experience. God came to him. Fox says:

> There is a trust implicit in the mystic's reliance on experience—
> a trust of the universe, a trust of what is and what occurs to us,
> yes, a trust of oneself. [You can argue that it wasn't God, that it
> was something else. But the mystic trusts that direct experience,
> that God does come.] As Meister Eckhart says, "Why is it that
> some people do not bear fruit? . . . Because they have no trust,
> either in God or in themselves. Love cannot distrust."[4]

Now God, the being of God, the presence of God, the numinous,
the holy, the ineffable is with us and in us every moment—the very
medium of our existence, just as water is the medium in which the fish
lives and swims. There is not a moment when we are not sustained and
held in existence by that presence. We forget God, but if God forgot
any one of us for a moment we would not be.

God thinks of us *every* moment, cherishes us, and delights in us in
every moment. No matter where we are, what we are thinking or
doing, that presence is beaming on us, enveloping us, longing to break
through.

This room is full of beams and sounds—beams which are carrying
images too numerous to count. We could bring in twenty TV sets and
place them around the room. There would be different channels, all of
which would be broadcasting simultaneously. All of these various
sounds and images are in this room this very moment. It is the television that receives and sends them out.

In like manner, the mystical consciousness is the instrument whereby
we receive into our deepest being the love that surrounds us, is seeking
to penetrate us and subsequently to radiate from us.

This love energy, this presence, this hope is inexhaustible. With God
there is no scarcity. The flow is infinite, never ending. "Take no
anxious thought for tomorrow." Why? Because what you need for
tomorrow will come in the inevitable flow.

"Consider the lilies of the field." Relax into God's infinite bounty.
You will be taken care of. You are safe. God is friendly. The manna will

flow. Deepen your connectedness with the unseen, real realm beyond this world.

In a meeting I recently attended one woman said, "You're talking about all this stuff, but we have to live out there in the real world." I said, "Let's talk a bit about what the real world is. If the world you are living in—the one you call the 'real world'-- *is* the real world, God help us all. I'm talking to you about the real world. You're talking about a very broken, distorted world."

We need to make deeper connections with the real world. We will then be sustained and nurtured every moment of our lives. We will live with a sense of awe and amazement and wonder and delight. The room where you now are is full of the Presence. All the rooms of your home throb with the Presence. You may not think it, but your work area, wherever you are, is throbbing with the Presence.

So tune in, and be carried. "They who wait for the LORD shall renew their strength, they shall mount up with wings like eagles, they shall run and not be weary, they shall walk and not faint" (Isa. 40:31, *RSV*).

God is very friendly, ever present. We can touch God, can connect at any moment. If we do not have the capacity to connect, we cannot connect. It is important that we learn to connect and to develop that mystical consciousness.

God is known not only directly; God comes to us in people. People are a part of our universe. So the question, "Is the universe friendly?" involves the question, "Are people friendly?" Many of us would like to consider these questions separately, saying, "Well, I can believe that God is friendly, but let's separate God from the people." But people happen to be a very important dimension through which the universe comes to us.

Are the people friendly? This is where the question gets extremely sticky. We know a little something about what happens when people are denied love. Children are abused, and later they become abusers. Rapists have often been raped. Hitler was beaten every day by his father, and he in turn beat millions of people. And with the help of millions of decent and educated people he exterminated six million Jews. These evidences of rampant evil in the world are not just in the past—not just "out there." They are right here—right in our city. Can you imagine how wounded one must be who spends his life deepening the addiction of a fellow human being to drugs? There are people in our city, in our neighborhoods, who are scheming constantly to strengthen their drug-marketing procedures in order to stay ahead of those who are trying to protect people from drugs and to help those already addicted to return to health. A very sophisticated marketing procedure developed by some very sharp minds is working hard so that people will become hooked.

A few days ago I met with a person who is working with this very issue. He said that the age group from seven to ten is now starting to use drugs. He is developing a kit with which parents can test their children to do away with the denial syndrome and the ignorance of parents as to whether their children are on drugs.

Are people friendly?

Just as we make a faith-decision concerning God and, by faith, say, "God is love; I will rest my weight on that love," we make a faith-decision regarding wounded, demonic people. The demonic comes into human life through wounded people. We know that everyone is wounded in some degree, and that all of us are limited in our capacity to love.

We make a faith-decision. The deepest essence of each of us is love. At bottom, we are made in God's image. God is love. I, you, every-one—is love. I will trust that inner revelation. I will treat people, all people, with love. Sensing God in their deeps, with my developed mystic consciousness, I will sense the numinous in them and will totally reverence them. Ultimately, we reverence everything or we reverence nothing.

By nature, by essence, we co-inhere with others. God is in them. If God's love and my love cannot touch the depths in the other, then I choose to take and absorb whatever may be directed toward me out of the evil of the other. That is far better than isolating myself, cutting myself off from God in people. The isolation technique is sure death. If I stay open, any hurt I sustain serves to drive me more deeply into God, who is love.

We sometimes seem to think that we are wiser than Jesus—that we know the world better than he knew it. But Jesus, more than any other, knew the nature of the demonic in people. With that knowledge and understanding he strode in love into the presence of the Gadarene demoniac and took his disciples with him. You can imagine their fear. But that demented one, who said that his name was "Legion," was integrated and made whole. Later, Jesus strode in love into the presence of the demonic embodied in the religious-military-industrial complex of his day, and for this he died. So in one case you have a healing, and in another case you have Jesus' death.

Today—two thousand years later—in Washington, D.C., in what is supposed to be the power center of the world, the power of dominance and the power of control—today we drink the blood that he shed for us.

Jesus, the world's greatest realist, believed the universe was friendly. So, even with what I know about the power of darkness and the demonic as it expresses itself through people, I am going to connect as Jesus did and let people—all people, my kind and not my kind—be the instruments of God's love and presence flowing into me. And I'm going to flow into them.

Let me say again that to connect is to relax. It is to rest. It is to trust. It is to let down. It is to be cared for. It is to be nourished.

For the most part, we are terribly isolated from people and we remain in a defensive stance toward those with whom we come in contact. To be alienated from people is to be alienated from God.

Perhaps our deepest alienation from God is our alienation from the creation. Strange, how completely most of us have been cut off from the creation. And how much violence we have perpetrated against her, this amazing created order that God has given us. Scripture says that the creation has been suffering, just as people have been suffering, because of our oppression.

"The created universe waits with eager expectation." . . . [It is longing to be freed. It is longing to be healed.] The universe itself is to be freed from the shackles of mortality. . . . Up to the present . . . the whole created universe groans in all its parts as if in the pangs of childbirth" (Rom. 8:19–23). This is the pain of the created order from which we have alienated ourselves.

A wonderful little book called *Shalom* by Ulrich Duchrow talks about the destruction that has been going on for a long, long time. He says, "Today's destruction of the environment differs from all the earlier destruction of the environment. Why? Because it is systematic, faster than the natural, regulating mechanisms of nature, and is worldwide in its dimensions."[5]

Duchrow lists some of the things which are happening: carbon dioxide in the atmosphere is steadily rising on the global scale. There are charts now of how many parts per million of carbon dioxide there are and, when they reach 350, the real changes begin to take place—the greenhouse effect. The figure in 1981 was 337. By now it is much larger.

These figures are directly tied to the rate of energy consumption. How much energy do we consume? How much do we extract? How much do we need? The ozone layer is still seriously endangered. The consequences of acid rain are worsening. Over-fishing of the waters in many areas is taking place. Pollution of coastal waters is increasing. There is a growing water shortage. Soil loss and deserts and the salinization of the soil are frequently being reported. And forests are being destroyed at an alarming rate.

The fate of the original tropical rainforests that God gave us is appalling. In East and West Africa 72 percent of our original rain forest has been destroyed. Yesterday a woman from Sierra Leone gave me a map, and looking at that map was a revelation for me. In Central Africa, 45 percent destroyed; in Latin America, 37 percent; in South Asia, 63 percent; in Southeast Asia, 38 percent. The world total is 42 percent. Gone already! And the destruction of the forests continues at such an unbelievable rate the imagination can scarcely conceive it.

We have been hostile to the creation. And just as we have tortured and continue to torture human beings (the work of Amnesty International attests to the way that has taken place around the world), and as we torture animals, we are also torturing subhuman and subanimal nature.

Bultmann, the great theologian, says the destruction of the outside environment corresponds to our illnesses within—what we call the diseases of civilization. To put things simply, each of us carries around the ecological crisis in our own bodies. Our task is to drop our hostility, our estrangement from the creation, and to begin to rest in it, to connect with it, to give it our friendship, to nurture it, to be nurtured by it, to meet God through it, to let God speak to us through it.

Ernesto Cardinale, the poet and revolutionary from Nicaragua, is a modern mystic. You can see, if you are a mystic, what you cannot see otherwise. In a little book called *To Live Is to Love*, he writes:

> All animals who sing at daybreak are singing for God. Volca-
> noes and the clouds and the trees speak to us of God in a loud
> voice. The entire creation proclaims resoundingly the existence
> and the beauty and the love of God. Music tells it to our ears

and the scenic beauty of nature conveys the message to our eyes. In all of nature we find God's initials, and all creatures are God's messages of love addressed to us.

All of nature burns with love created through love to light love in us. Nature is like a shadow of God, a reflection of His beauty. The blue of the placid lake mirrors this divine splendor. In every atom an image of the Trinity is enshrined, a faint resemblance of the triune God. My entire body, too, has been made to love God. Each of its cells is a hymn to the Creator and a continuous declaration of love.[6]

Where do we start? Duchrow says we might start with the breath that we breathe. That is where we connect most intimately every moment with the created order. He writes:

Whenever created beings inhale, they receive new life. And we receive God's breath. Inhaling is normally passive. Whoever draws breath in this way breathes wrongly, for this is taking God's gift for oneself. Whoever pauses before inhaling, experiences it as an overwhelming gift. "We are ever being created anew," says the psalmist. Therefore, we can do nothing. No one can bring him/herself into the world. We are born into it. At the end of inhaling we experience a high point, much like reaching the top of a hill. And the downhill is the exhalation. That is active. When exhaling we must consciously breathe out fully. It is difficult, since when exhaling we must surrender life, because what was built up in us when inhaling is released again. We must be prepared to give things up. To pour ourselves out. To inspire others. In every exhalation we must die a little.[7]

Courage and confidence come with exhaling. Will they result in new inhaling? That cannot be taken for granted. That we always find new breath—that we are always created anew—these are miracles. Were you aware of that this morning? Or did you just passively breathe without thinking about it at all?

Connecting every moment. Every mist that settles upon the earth, we draw from. We see it, we connect with it. Every time the sky is beautiful, every time it rains, every tree that we see, every flower that we look at.

If we are connecting directly with God, with God through people, with God through the universe, there is not a moment that we are not being renewed—not just during our sixty minutes at the beginning of the day. Everywhere we go we are picking up messages. We are renewed. We are excited. We stand in awe. And everyone we see, no matter how distorted and broken that person is, that person feeds us. We relax into and are safe with that person.

The universe is there all the time, in every breath you breathe, in every step you take, and in everything you look at. If we are connected, the universe is a part of us. And we are respecting it, loving it, revering it.

If we can live this way, then death is a most simple passage. We just go from this friendly dimension to the next friendly dimension. And it will be a wondrous and beautiful experience.

Notes

[1] Matthew Fox, *The Coming of the Cosmic Christ* (New York: Harper Collins, 1988), p. 11.

[2] Ibid.

[3] Ibid., p. 49.

[4] Ibid.

[5] Ulrich Duchrow and Gerhard Liedke, *Shalom* (Geneva: WCC Publications, 1989), p. 16.

[6] Ernesto Cardinale, *To Live Is to Love*, trans. Kurt Reinhardt (Garden City, N.Y.: Image Books, 1974), pp. 29–30.

[7] Duchrow and Liedke, *Shalom*, p. 16.

18

Pain, Power, and the Poor

This 1990 homily relates our inner pain, the biblical understanding of power, and the importance of becoming connected in a real way with the poor.

The Scripture commonly known as the Fourth Servant Poem of Isaiah reads:

> Behold, my servant shall prosper,
> he shall be lifted up, exalted to the heights.
>
> Time was when many were aghast at you, my people;
> so now many nations recoil at sight of him,
> and kings curl their lips in disgust.
> For they see what they had never been told
> and things unheard before fill their thoughts.
>
> Who could have believed what we have heard,
> and to whom has the power of the Lord been revealed?
>
> He [the Servant] grew up before the LORD like a young
> plant
> whose roots are in parched ground;
> he had no beauty, no majesty to draw our eyes,
> no grace to make us delight in him;
> his form, disfigured, lost all the likeness of a man,
> his beauty changed beyond human semblance.
> He was despised, he shrank from the sight of men,
> tormented and humbled by suffering;
> we despised him, we held him of no account,
> a thing from which men turn away their eyes.

> Yet, on himself he bore our sufferings,
>   our torments he endured,
> while we counted him smitten by God,
>   struck down by disease and misery;
> but he was pierced for our transgressions,
>   tortured for our iniquities;
> the chastisement he bore is health for us,
>   and by his scourging we are healed. (Isa. 52:13—53:5)

Our New Testament Scripture is found in the thirteenth chapter of John's Gospel:

> It was before the Passover festival. Jesus knew that his hour had come and he must leave this world and go to the Father. He had always loved his own who were in the world, and now he was to show the full extent of his love.
>
> The devil had already put it into the mind of Judas son of Simon Iscariot to betray him. During supper, Jesus, well aware that the Father had entrusted everything to him, and that he had come from God and was going back to God [That is the prelude. To do what he did, you really have to know that you have come from God and are going back to God.], rose from the table, laid aside his garments, and taking a towel, tied it round him. Then he poured water into a basin, and began to wash his disciples' feet and to wipe them with the towel. [This was very distressing to Simon Peter, because it just didn't fit the image he had of his Lord.]
>
> When it was Simon Peter's turn, Peter said to him, 'You, Lord, washing my feet?" [You're not going to wash my feet. It's not appropriate. That is not who you are.] Jesus replied, "You do not understand now what I am doing, but one day you will." Peter said, "I will never let you wash my feet." "If I do not wash you," Jesus replied, "you are not in fellowship with me." "Then, Lord," said Simon Peter, "not my feet only; wash my hands and head as well!" . . .
>
> After washing their feet and taking his garments again, he sat down. "Do you understand what I have done for you?" he asked. "You call me 'Master' and 'Lord,' and rightly so, for that is what I am. [But I want you to get a different idea of what it means to be Master and Lord.] Then if I, your Lord and Master, have washed your feet, you also ought to wash one another's feet. I have set you an example: you are to do as I have done for you. In very truth I tell you, a servant is not greater than his master, nor a messenger than the one who sent him. If you know this, happy are you if you act upon it." (vv. 1–17)

Hearing it just doesn't make any difference. But happy are you if you really get it, if you internalize it, if you are able to act on it.

When God is present in any depth in a people, something new will break forth. God, by nature, is one who does a "new thing." And a mark of the Holy Spirit is newness. Wherever Jesus was, newness was always breaking loose. Bodies were healed, spirits were elevated, energy was released, sin was forgiven, hope and excitement were everywhere evident. These are the reasons everybody wanted to be around Jesus. All these things happen here and now when we are truly the people of God, the community of faith.

For individuals, there are *kairos* moments, and there is *kronos* time. Kronos time is time that just goes on. Henri Nouwen says this sort of time is opaque. Nothing from beyond breaks in. We talk about chronology; kronos time is ordinary time. We live most of our time in kronos time. It just goes on and on and on.

But when time is transparent—in kairos time—the beyond breaks through. The holy, the numinous is present in that moment and everything is different. We are touched in our depths. We experience the extraordinary. Another dimension is present in that moment.

One of the reasons we keep retelling the episodes in the life of Jesus is simply because these are accounts of kairos time. Jesus was abiding so deeply in the One whom he called Abba, that Abba was always breaking in, always speaking to him, always doing something through him. So kairos is a time of special breakthrough, when the ineffable breaks in. There is no adequate way to describe it. There are no adequate images to describe the real world, which is beyond this world. We think of that as the ephemeral, the pious world, and we keep saying, "How is this going to work in the real world?" Well, that is the real world. We are not trained to touch that world with any consistency, because we are too developed in the left brain, and the mystic consciousness is experienced through the right brain. Patrick Cavanaugh says, "God cannot catch us unless we stay in the unconscious room of our hearts."

Although we are not trained to touch that real world with any consistency, most of us have hints of those experiences that we call kairos moments.

This kind of experience happens not just to individuals but also to communities—to nations—and to various sections of the world. It seems to be happening in South Africa. It seems to be happening in

Europe. And as President Havel said to Congress, "There are not any speedometers you can measure it with, because it's happening so rapidly."

A breakthrough from God can come to a congregation, to a parish, to a whole people. A people can experience a kairos moment, a kairos period. Fresh energy flows, corporate depression is lifted, many persons are touched by the divine. As Moses' face shone when he came down from the mountain, the corporate face of a congregation can begin to shine with deep joy.

An angel comes and troubles the corporate waters. The people recognize themselves as truly being members of one another—having a deep co-inherence. This is not something that we pull off by our own exhausting efforts but something that God does. People begin to rest, and then to swim in this ocean of love. A kairos moment or period is given, and a whole people is forever different, just as an individual is different when that individual has been invaded from the beyond.

To be in touch with the Beyond is what we really want—to be aware of the Presence. Three dimensions of preparation are to be emphasized as we wait for God's presence.

In considering these dimensions, let us remember the paradox. On the one hand, the presence of the Spirit and the conscious sense of that Spirit in the community are always gift—gift which never comes simply as a consequence of our faithful efforts. "The wind blows where it wills"—always sheer gift, always mystery.

The other side of the paradox is that the gift can be prepared for. We can seek to understand the nature of God and the nature of the waiting. We cannot ensure the gift. We cannot demand it. The minute we shift over to demand we lose the receptive frame of heart that we need. But we wait with prepared hearts, with a sense of eagerness and expectation that it will be given. I have seen it happen so many times that I cannot be skeptical now. I just know it happens.

As for the three extremely important preparatory steps—we talk a lot about them in our community, but we have not learned fully to implement them. None of the three can be omitted if we are to live out of this other ineffable transcendental dimension of life.

First, we have to get in touch with and deal with our inner pain. We have to find a place for the processing of pain. I am convinced that the church must be a place where people can share their pain. The pain of all of us is overwhelming. No one escapes. And if we can develop a level of trust in one another so that we begin to tell our stories, we will find that there is always pain in those stories.

Robert Coles has written a book called *The Call of Stories*. He is working with people who are attending business school and medical school at Harvard. He talks about the power of stories, and how we need to be able to share our stories with one another.

One night in the Potter's House (a Christian coffee house started by The Church of the Saviour in 1960), I was sitting with four people that I thought I knew fairly well. Something happened to change the feeling and people began to talk. I found that three of these four women had been sexually abused when they were children. And they were talking about it.

This is what AA is all about: the telling of personal stories. In AA and Al-Anon and Co-dependents Anonymous and Adult Children of Alcoholic Parents, and drug recovery centers—on and on it goes—people telling their stories and sharing their pain.

Often we feel that our own personal pain is unique. We feel cut off. But when at last we can share it, when we can tell our stories to those who themselves are in pain and who really want to hear them, healing begins.

The strange thing is that the church, which is by definition a place of healing, is often the place where it is most difficult to share our pain. I frequently meet with groups of clergy, and I often find them to be the loneliest people I know. For the most part, they have no place to share their pain.

Inner pain must be brought to speech if there is to be healing. *Cry Pain, Cry Hope* is the title of a book by Elizabeth O'Connor of our own staff and our own community. She has established a number of compassion groups where deep pain can be shared and heard, and healing can begin. There are now three of these groups under the auspices of the Servant Leadership School. Elizabeth would strongly urge everyone to find his or her wailing wall.

Strange, isn't it, that although the church is by definition the place of healing, most of the groups that are springing up—literally thousands of them—are outside the church. These groups, which give people opportunity to tell their stories, are bursting at the seams. There is a center here at Dupont Circle. They are all over this city. They are all over the country. A recent issue of *Newsweek* estimates that approximately fifteen million people across the country are supported by this type of group.

I would hope that we could move from the concept of processing our pain to creating structures for the processing for those who have this hunger.

Not only does healing occur in the sharing of pain, but community develops as we share our hurt, our weaknesses, our brokenness, our woundedness. We feel closer to one another as we become vulnerable in the sharing of our weaknesses, rather than in the parading of our strengths. No experiencing of pain, no healing. No mutual experiencing of pain, no deep community.

So the first "P" is finding a place to process our *pain*. This is a part of the preparation for the breakthrough of the kairos. As long as we are insulated from our own pain, God has an almost impossible time breaking through.

The second absolutely essential step in preparation for this newness, for being a kairos decade, for being a spectacular decade, is the inner shifting of the nature of power.

The biblical understanding of power is fundamentally different from the world's understanding. The world worships the power of dominance, control, prestige, status, influence, money—the power of effectiveness, getting things done. With this kind of power, greed is the consuming disease. We even seek to garner this sort of power to use it on behalf of the oppressed and the poor and the marginal people of the world. But in garnering it on behalf of the poor, we still have the power.

Ultimate power is the giving away of power—total renunciation of this kind of power. The supreme image for us is the image of the lamb that was slain from the foundation of the world—the slain Lamb. Interestingly enough, the image of Jesus, the dominant image in the book of Revelation depicting the events after this world is terminated, is still the slain Lamb.

Dorothy Soelle talks about Siegfried, the German male hero. He was the one who killed the dragon that was wreaking such destruction. After he had killed it, he bathed in the dragon's blood. The myth indicated that this made him invincible and invulnerable. Most of us are trying to bathe in the blood of the dragon and not in the blood of the Lamb. In fact, we're a little uneasy when we talk about the blood of the Lamb.

Jimilu Mason's "Servant Christ" in front of Christ House depicts the Christ who took the towel and a basin and washed the feet of the disciples. The Jesus of this sculpture is at street level, looking into the eyes of the homeless, sick people of the city—the people who are being served by Christ House. This is a tremendously compelling piece. I like to sit there and watch the people as they connect with that vulnerable Christ. They do all sorts of things to him. The criticism is often voiced, "This figure should be elevated. It should be protected. It should not be at street level." But Jesus says, "I am among you as one who serves." And that is the ultimate power.

Our task over a lifetime is to change our inner power base and our conception of power. We brought the Servant Leadership School into being to work primarily with this difficult issue. I think on the whole the church is as enamored with dominating, controlling power as are the business and political communities. We do not trust the power of love, the power of serving, the power of vulnerability, the power of the cross. We are embarrassed by the blood of the slain Lamb. Yet this is the image of Jesus which is central to Scripture, and it is perhaps our most neglected image.

The first recorded command that Jesus gives is "Repent, for the kingdom of heaven is at hand" (Matt. 4:17, *RSV*). And we turn that into a moral sort of repentance. I think what Jesus is saying is, "Change the way you look at life. Change your whole way of responding to it because this kingdom, this transcendent world, this other real world is at hand and is ready to break in upon you. All you have to do is to change the way you see things." Repent, in this sense, and it will break in.

When this inner change occurs and the other kingdom breaks in, this change literally transforms the whole value system. All need for protection leaves. There is a welcoming of total vulnerability. I'm happy to go wherever the flow takes me; the unknown, the new, is no longer frightening. I don't need anything because abundance is all around. I'm totally safe in the unseen, bathed in this perfect love. There's no room for fear. All desire to extract from the common good is gone; rather, one simply wants to give, give, give; to serve in whatever lowly, unspectacular way is available in love. A sense of meaning and empowerment comes through loving and serving.

In the biblical sense such profound inner change is repentance. Jesus was talking about this when he said, "You must be born again."

In this deep sense there are not many "born-again Christians" walking around with a change in their inner sense of what power is.

We first considered the preparing of structures for the processing of pain. The second "P" step of preparation has concerned the shifting over inwardly to God's conception of *power*—literally renouncing the world's power as Jesus did in the temptation stories.

The third step of preparation is to become intimately connected with the poor. Something happens to us when we actually connect with the poor, something that cannot happen when we refuse to know that wounded, broken, repulsive person out there. Merely seeing that person and feeling that person to be a part of my own body are two widely different experiences.

One chilly morning as I walked down Columbia Road I saw a woman sitting on some newspapers with her back against a brick wall. She was a most unprepossessing sight. Her head was tied up in a stained, dirty scarf from which strands of matted hair protruded. She was clothed in a ragged, dark dress and had a small blanket around her shoulders. A quote attributed to Mother Teresa flashed through my mind: "Here is Jesus in another distressing disguise."

As I dropped a bill into her cup, she looked up at me out of red-rimmed eyes and murmured, "I'm hungry." That night, on my way to my comfortable, clean bed, I thought of her and wondered where she was spending the night. Should I have offered to help her to her feet, walked with her to a nearby McDonald's Restaurant, and sat with, and spoken with her as she ate? What a lot we have to learn about how best to relate to the children of God who are living in such abject poverty.

There is a deep connection between the touching of our own pain and our touching the acute pain of the other, the one who has "no form nor comeliness," which is what the fifty-third chapter of Isaiah is saying. Someone might say, "How can I know joy if I let the world's suffering into my heart?" The truth is, one can never know authentic joy unless one embraces that suffering and enters into it deeply. Intimate belonging to the poor is a rare achievement. Having a poor person as an intimate friend is very unusual. Serving the poor is more frequent, though still too rare. But the intimacy and the closeness take a lot of time—time that most of us choose not to give because the things we are already doing are too "important." We don't see the necessity of this intimacy.

When we do take the time, radical internal changes occur. David Hilfiker, in *Not All of Us Are Saints,* describes with vivid authenticity the difficult inner passages that he underwent during a six-year period. He moved inwardly as he began to know this sort of intimacy.

How difficult it is for us to realize how big the chasm is between the Gospel vision and what most of us feel—what most people in our society feel—at the point of the poor.

A minister came to see me a few weeks ago. He brought with him the senior warden of his congregation and the former senior warden. He wanted to talk about the possibility of his church's being connected with the poor. They were thinking about the possibility of taking care of a meal at Christ House or some similar shelter in the city.

After visiting with these three people, I said, "I could very easily work out a place and a structure for you to serve in that way. But let me suggest another possibility. Why don't you bring a group here—just ten or fifteen of your people? We can take a day and talk about the theology of mission and of being with the poor. We can also talk about the inner life, how you hear call, and about how you can really get connected with the poor." They thought that might be a good way to proceed and that it would have greater depth than just coming in to work in a soup kitchen. Then I said, "Let's take a few minutes to wander around the neighborhood." In just one hour we had this conversation, and we wandered around the neighborhood.

The pastor said that they were going to have a retreat and decide what to do. I didn't hear from him for several weeks, so I called him up. He said, "You know, I really am interested. I want this to happen. But the people that I brought with me are still in a state of shock." One hour put those people from that suburban congregation in a state of shock! They simply could not understand a world so different from the one in which they live.

We are trying now to build a racially, culturally, economically balanced church, the Festival Church, which is an offspring of the Jubilee Church. We are finding this a very difficult thing to do. Normally, blacks do their things, and the Hispanic folk do their things, and we whites do ours. Moreover, even within the racial groups the differences economically make being together in a church very threatening.

Why is it so hard to be with the poor when Jesus was so often with the poor and made it so clear that God loves the poor? We say we long to be with Jesus. We want to deepen that connection. Surely one thing is obvious: if we are going to be intimate friends of persons who are very poor we will have to question the degree of wealth that we cling to. In the preparation that we are making for kairos it is very clear that Jesus has to be obeyed. "If you love me, you will keep my commandments" (John 14:15, *RSV*).

So these would be the three P's: processing our own inner *pain*, working with our own conception of *power* and trying to shift it over so that what gives us joy are the basin and the towel—not the prestige, the status, and the upward mobility. (The thing that gives us real joy is that we have been diminished.) And finally, connecting deeply with the *poor*.

As we work with these concerns, amazing things will begin to happen. God's beneficent manna will begin falling all over the place. We won't have time to pick it up. Person after person will begin to have an inner response to some area of acute need. And everybody will be responding to the need, saying, "Let me do it. I feel called." Instead of vainly hoping that a call may be heard once every six months, there will be calls all over the place.

A heightened sense of community will be experienced—closeness, intimacy, deep belonging. There will be energy, vitality, excitement, awe. People looking at this church will see not an institution or an organization. They will see a family—a family of faith, of love, of compassion. They will see God's face.

"Behold," says God, "I do a new thing." Can you see it?

19

March for Freedom in Selma

~

This reflection was written in 1965, upon Gordon's return to Washington from the civil-rights march in Selma, Alabama.

On March 9, 1965, Dr. Martin Luther King, Jr., of the Southern Christian Leadership Conference led the Freedom March in Selma, Alabama. As one of more than forty ministers from the Washington area I went on a chartered flight to Selma to participate in that event.

Before recording what I sensed of the mood in Selma as a result of what happened there, I want to express appreciation of what was for me personally the most meaningful dimension of the week. Never before have I felt the support of my community as I did in those stressful days. Spontaneous expressions of closeness and love came through to me in countless little and big ways for which I am deeply grateful.

As the backdrop for consideration of the Freedom March, let us keep in mind the Scripture: "He was wounded for our transgressions, he was bruised for our iniquities; upon him was the chastisement that made us whole, and with his stripes we are healed" (Isa. 53:5, *RSV*).

The flight to Selma was an uneventful trip, but there was a sense of expectancy, of tenseness. As we left the plane, we were told it would be possible to have dinner in the Montgomery airport. However, when we entered the airport and were met by the veterans of the Freedom Movement, it was immediately obvious that there would be no lingering. In an atmosphere thick with tension we were hurried into cars, pickup trucks, and micro-buses. Our driver, an art teacher in a Mississippi college, had come to Selma with his wife, who was about to have a baby. Most of the freedom workers, whenever they move from place to place, will take off at any moment, any night, in order to be a part of the movement and make their contribution. In this way our driver was waiting for his baby to be born.

Another occupant of the car was a sixteen-year-old boy, Theophilus Bailey, a SNCC worker who had been active in the movement for two years. We were told that we could expect anything, and that down the road a few miles there was a highway control point. Sure enough, ten minutes later we were stopped. We were asked our point of origin, our destination, and the purpose of the trip. Meantime a man was seen writing down the license number of the car.

As we proceeded in caravan, ominous looking cars and trucks passed by with short-wave radio antennae. A few minutes later Theophilus, who was the most aware of what was happening, asked whether anyone in the car had a knife. Yes, there were one or two pocket knives. He immediately instructed us to get rid of them, because if we were stopped we would be accused of having concealed weapons. Then he asked again: "Any other weapons or anything which could be construed as a weapon?" Yes, the artist had a long file which he used in his art. He hesitated to throw it out; it would cost money to replace it, and he needed it. Money is scarce in Alabama. So for the rest of the trip I held the file—ready to dispose of it instantly if we were stopped. Theophilus further enlightened us concerning the technicalities of Alabama law, with the final instruction to let him out quickly if we were stopped; he would fade away into the night so we would not be charged with contributing to the delinquency of minors.

The bridge was a crucial point—the place where trouble was most likely to occur. This bridge spanned the Alabama River over which the marchers had trudged just the day before. Here the tear gas had been thrown and some in the crowd had panicked, especially the children. Horses had trampled helpless victims, and the troopers and posse had beaten women, children, and men. From this point the marchers had been beaten and whipped back like cattle to Brown's Chapel. All was quiet when we crossed, with only a few state troopers and their patrol cars in evidence.

Several minutes later we arrived at Brown's Chapel, where a mass meeting was being held in preparation for the march on Tuesday. We passed through the police cars guarding the area, thanked our driver, and pushed through the milling, singing crowd into the church—a moment to remember forever. We were the first contingent of what was to be wave after wave of white clergymen from all over the nation. The church was jammed, with three balconies filled, every aisle full, the choir full, and hundreds of people standing outside. I don't know how the church remained intact with those frail balconies so loaded and with all that sound and movement. An elderly woman struck up the tune:

> Mine eyes have seen the glory of the coming of the Lord.
> He is trampling out the vintage where the grapes of wrath
>   are stored.
> He has loosed the fateful lighting of his terrible swift
>   sword—
> His truth is marching on![1]

Never have I heard that hymn sung as it was sung that night, and in that moment I knew it was right that we were there. You could see hope written on those faces lined with suffering—and the feeling, "Tomorrow we shall not walk alone. There are others to share our suffering." Later that night as we sat and talked, my host and I, in a simple little home, he said to me, "Tonight was the most beautiful sight I've ever seen in my life, when you walked in." He said, "I'd have given up my place in glory to see that sight." I think this is the way most of the people felt.

The representatives of our group brought greetings to the Selma people. Many songs were sung, and finally, about eleven o'clock, Martin Luther King, Jr., with Ralph Abernathy, James Farmer, and a host of others arrived. Their speeches were most moving. Shortly after midnight (many times they had stayed all night, and would have then had it been necessary) they sang the closing song, "We Shall Overcome," in a way that was profoundly touching.

Some things I had known with my mind before, but now I knew them with my emotions. The first was this: The Spirit had descended upon the black church of Jesus Christ in the Black Belt of the South. That church, the black church, had found its mission—tackling the principalities and powers in the high places. The Holy Spirit was there.

I knew another thing: There was no stopping this movement. The walls of segregation were cracking, and these people would not stop until together they had crumbled them. I felt shame for the society that you and I have helped to perpetuate, but I also felt a deep sense of pride for this new generation of Americans. In spite of the anguish aroused in me by this unbelievable system which enslaves the bodies and souls of people, I felt great pride that here was America—a new America. You can put it down in the record that the Negro is no longer scared. He is afraid in the way I am afraid, and he is afraid as you would be in the midst of danger, but he is not scared as he used to be scared.

Some of the most meaningful hours of my trip were spent in the home of those who looked after me that night. We were not able to work out the arrangements as planned, because more people than were expected came and most homes were filled.

As we approached his little shack, I said to my host, "I would be glad to sleep on the floor if that is all right, or I can sleep in your car."

He said, "Don't you worry, we'll look after you." We talked for a while and I learned something about the way the Negroes in Selma live. I sat on a chair which was bent far backward. He apologized, brought me another chair and said, "You know we ordered a set of kitchen furniture and it has come but we're scared to get it."

I said, "What do you mean?"

"Well, just the other day a friend of mine went into a store to buy something and they started beating him. The way he got out was through the plate-glass window. Even if we made it as far as the white merchants of the city are concerned, I wouldn't dare do it on account of the Freedom Movement. You see, we are boycotting the stores, and if they found me picking up this item, the Freedom leaders would be after me. I couldn't make it either way."

The domestic workers get ten to twelve dollars a week. Some of them work from 7 A.M. to 7 P.M., five or six days a week. This means, of course, that mothers have to work, and the men often have to work two jobs. The woman in the family left next morning at 6:30 to make the trek of thirty-five miles to the factory where she would put labels on salt and pepper containers.

We stopped talking about 2 A.M., but it must have been nearly an hour before the household finally settled down. The whole city was tense; the home was tense and the children, of course, were awake. Children feel the anxiety, and I heard the parents comforting them and talking to them about the morrow. Whether anyone slept or not, I do not know, but at 5:00 A.M. the lights were on and everything was alive and active.

I had slept in the living room on the sofa. In this little bit of time from 5:00 to 6:30 I saw as beautiful a piece of family life as I have ever watched, characterized by the respect of the parents for each other and for their children, and of the children for their parents, and the resulting very evident teamwork.

Eleven-year-old Ferdinand prepared lunches for all five children, then fixed his mother's lunch. He dressed, gathered his books together, looked over his assignments, scrambled the eggs, fixed the hominy grits, and served the breakfast. All this time the mother was braiding the hair of the girls. I never knew it took fifteen minutes to braid the hair of one little girl, and there were three of them—forty-five minutes.

Only one family crisis occurred. Little five-year-old Louise, with her spindly legs, wanted to go on the march, but they would not let her go. The amazing thing is that she knew some of the implications of what would happen. Children know. You can criticize the movement for having children in the forefront. The problem is that you cannot stop them. At 6:30 the mother left and the father took the children to the place where they were to stay until school time. Ferdinand washed the dishes and the home was neat and clean by seven o'clock.

Then we went to the church for the morning rally. We were taught how to protect ourselves when committed to nonviolence. First of all, there's the tear gas. Amazing to learn that, when they throw tear gas on you, you run into it. You don't run away; you find out which way the wind is blowing and you move into it, because the gas will follow you if you try to run away from it. They ask you not to panic. They tell you, however, that they know you will panic. Then they tell you what position to get in when you're being beaten with a billy club. Your head is what is important—nothing else matters; so you find ways to protect your head. Then you are told that if you are a man, you are to fling your body over a woman if she is being beaten. Said one leader, "We'll not have our women beaten until they have beaten all the men."

An ethical issue arose. Someone wanted to know if it would be all right to play dead after they've beaten you, so they'll quit. I think the consensus was that it was all right to play dead, even if a bit deceptive. Next came the dramatic time when we argued the wisdom of violating a federal injunction. Then we were reminded of the commitment to nonviolence. The majority of the leadership as well as the people are really committed to nonviolence, but only for the present. I don't know how long this will hold true—it is one of the issues.

One of the clergymen asked, "If they are beating us, may we grab the billy stick?" The sixteen-year-old who was briefing this group of bishops and other clergy said, "Absolutely not. That is exactly the excuse they are waiting for. If you are unable to keep from grabbing the billy stick, don't you go on this march." He said, "If you've got any switchblades on you, if you've got any pistols, throw them into the nearest garbage can. I've thought about this many times, and I'm perfectly willing to die. In fact, I didn't know why I was born until this came along and I became a part of it, and now I know why I was born. I'm willing to die, but I'm not going to die because of no switchblade."

Then came the charge to the adults—the first time I've heard a teenager charge adults. He said, "Everyone knows that the students are the backbone of this movement, but the backbone is not much good without some flesh. You adults are the flesh. Today when we are on this march I want you adults to behave like adults." He said, "The children and even the teenagers panic first. But you have lived longer than the rest of us and you ought to know how to deport yourselves. You act like adults this afternoon because we need you."

After this came the preparation of the crowd for Martin Luther King's death, should this occur. We heard a surgeon had been flown to Atlanta just in case. To prepare the crowd, it was made known that there was leadership which would carry on and the movement would not stop.

Then King appeared—a young Moses ready to lead his people. For him, Pharaoh had said no, and God had said yes. King said, "I would rather die on the highways of Alabama than live with a butchered conscience." I have a new appreciation for King and for the stature of the man, and I have a new appreciation for the complexities and the problems of leadership. To coldly calculate, a thousand miles away, the logical steps for King to take is one thing. But it is quite another thing to determine the right steps to take in the midst of passionate thousands some of whom fear that the moves taken are not sufficiently daring—who even question the whole idea of nonviolence and would like to wrench the movement into their own violent hands.

About the march itself. Three or four thousand people left the church with King, Abernathy, and Farmer in the lead, with some of the most important white clergy in the country in the front. The rest of the white clergy were scattered throughout all the crowd; the strategy was that when they beat they would have to beat everybody. Even Governor Wallace and James Clark and Mayor Smitherman would not want to beat Mrs. Paul Douglas (wife of the Senator from Illinois) if they could help it.

On the plane back I was talking with a Negro minister friend and he said, "You know, I've never been so scared in all my life. What about you?"

I said, "I've been more scared a few times, but I did have a new feeling. I've never felt before that I was going intentionally into a trap, watching the exits close and knowing there was no way of getting back. You couldn't get out to the east or the west or the north or the south. They would drive you back this path with every exit closed—back to the Brown Chapel. The feeling I'd never known before was that in the springing of the trap there was nothing you could do; you were committed ahead of time to doing nothing." I've gone into many a difficult situation which there was no way to avoid but, once in it, I fought my way out. Here you were committed to doing nothing rather than violate the witness.

The fear was so great that even the townspeople were not speaking. Not a word. Not a single derogatory remark did I hear. One sentence, you felt, could set it off. What admiration I felt for Negroes who live in that community and who will be there in the months to come! Here they were, going back on Tuesday, on the same line of march they had followed Sunday. I do not know how they did it. A teenage boy, when we got to the bridge, said to his companion, "Let's go home." He walked a few feet and then came back and joined the crowd. A human barricade of state troopers lined the way, one every fifty feet, and cars were going back and forth. Then came the prayer meeting, with three or four thousand people kneeling on the highway. King said there had never been such a mass meeting on the highways of Alabama, whites and blacks together.

Finally, we turned around and went back. There was one sign of hope, which I didn't see, but my host did. He saw a state trooper standing there with tears streaming down his face, a sight that could break the heart of even the most hardened. The ones I saw did not look that way.

One who has been to Selma will never forget Selma. What you saw there was a group of people who are being wounded for our transgressions, who are being bruised for our iniquities. You get a new appreciation of the people of God. Selma is a symbol—it is every community in our nation. Washington is Selma, too. Be ready to go to Selma, to Montgomery, to wherever people in the nation care. If need be, let us set aside twenty-eight hundred dollars from our Easter offering to charter a plane, to have it on a moment's notice to go where we need to go. The battleground will shift. It is Selma today; it will be Montgomery next week. But the real battleground for most of us is Washington. Here the needs are as acute in their way as the needs in Selma.

Junior Village [an institution for dependent children] should be eliminated. Almost one thousand children there are being denied what every child must have, and we sit around and watch, just as the citizens in Germany sat around and watched the fate of millions in the concentration camps and the gas chambers. We wonder how they did it—and we are doing it.

The slums of our city must go. A civilization which fails to respect all of its citizens will end up respecting none of them. The slums will never go until Washington is an open city and God's children can live anywhere. More power to those who have been faithfully working at the fair-housing drive presently going on.

Let us find our mission, each of us; and let us march and sing until we overcome. The nation is flocking to Selma because simple people in the Black Belt have found their mission and are willing to suffer and die. I want to extend this challenge to our teenagers. A Negro teenager challenged me to behave like an adult in Selma, and I would like to challenge you to live with God until you find that some segment of the city is laid on your heart and you'll not rest until you help make it whole. You will lay down your life if need be.

A word concerning the significance of time: If justice moves too slowly (and make no mistake, it has been moving too slowly) the more violent will be listened to by the people and for a time our nation will know a reign of terror. The blood of blacks and whites will mingle in the streets because we refuse to mingle in life. Tomorrow a voting bill goes to Congress. Pray. Write your Congressman. Go to see him. Let the Congress know that the citizens are aroused, and all God's children must vote.

Let us no longer take counsel with our fears. Let us decide that we will do the right thing, not the expedient thing. Time is of the essence. For God's sake find your mission. Come to grips with the meaning of death. Let us come to the place that we are willing to die. With the violence that is being created in our nation, we may not live anyway, and we might as well die as we seek to "let justice roll down like waters."

Note

[1] "The Battle Hymn of the Republic," *The United Methodist Hymnal* (Nashville, Tenn.: The United Methodist Publishing Company, 1982), p. 171.

20

Crusade for Captive Children

❧

*This reflection was written in 1963, during the Civil Rights Move-
ment. It led to the formation of For Love of Children, FLOC, an
organization that has continued to advocate for dependent children.*

To be in the midst of the Freedom Movement, as expressed in the
black church in the Black Belt, is to touch a spirit and to go away
changed. This is the common testimony of those who have been there.
Here a new America is emerging; here is a new spirit of freedom. The
leaders make it plain that theirs is a worldwide missionary cause. They
say that after the South there is Harlem, and after Harlem there is
Vietnam, and after Vietnam there is the Congo—wherever people are
oppressed, there they will be. With this dramatic expression of what it
means to belong to him who is the Suffering Servant, we can see what
it means to enter into the passion and death of Jesus Christ, to assume
the form of a servant.

We are in a time of reexamining what it means to be a people on
mission. We are rethinking the discipline which describes our shape as
it relates to mission. We must constantly renew the symbols and the
understandings by which we live.

Three ways of thinking which are deeply rooted in a biblical understanding of the church are dramatically illustrated in the Freedom
Movement. They are; identification with the outcast, a total commitment, and a corporate witness.

❧ *Identification with the Outcast* ❧

In the words of Dietrich Bonhoeffer, "The mission of the church is to
participate in God's suffering in a Godless world."[1] And in the words of

Albert Van den Heuvel, "The task of the church is to be awake with Jesus."[2] You remember, in the Garden of Gethsemane Jesus asked the disciples to stay awake and pray with him. He went a short distance apart and prayed. When he returned and found them asleep, he asked, "Could none of you stay awake with me one hour?" (Matt. 26:41).

The task of the church is to participate in the powerlessness of God where his power is least evident, to be present among the suffering, carrying their sorrow, choosing to be with the outlawed. "Only he," says Bonhoeffer, "who shouts for the Jews is allowed to use Gregorian Chants."[3] The story of Jesus is that of one who shared people's lives—not just their flesh. At his birth he shared the homelessness of the conscripted. He shared the isolation of the tax-gatherer, the loneliness of the excommunicated sinner, the temptation to make things visible and to call for miracles. He shared the death of the criminal. In this process of sharing he endures our temptation and our death, and frees us from our loneliness and our guilt.

Those who belong to Jesus, who comprise the church, are to stand with the outcast, the downtrodden, the outlawed, and the dispossessed. When Jesus described his own mission and gave the reason he came, he selected this passage from Isaiah:

> The spirit of the Lord is upon me because he has anointed
>   me;
> he has sent me to announce good news to the poor,
> to proclaim release for prisoners and recovery of sight for
>   the blind;
> to let the broken victims go free,
> to proclaim the year of the Lord's favour. (Lk 4:18–19)

He thus identified his mission, which is also the mission of the church. The church is to be identified with care for the poor, for those who are on the relief rolls, and for the criminals and outcasts.

When the chips are down, how few people really care about the poor, how few want to be with them. A society which is not concerned for its poor cannot be healthy. The question comes to me again and again: why is it so difficult to choose for the outcast? Consciously, as Christians, we are committed to the outcast. But volitionally and emotionally, why do we have such trouble? Is it because the outcast is always a dramatic reminder of society's failure and, consequently, of our own failure to do battle with the principalities and powers—to do battle with the structures of poverty, of unemployment, sordid housing, and the hopelessness and the hatred which they always breed? Is it that we are unable to face our own guilt, for we have been willing to profit by structures which have degraded others? The system has favored us, so we have been unwilling to rock the boat. Any attempt to deal basically with the existing system we have quickly labeled communism, or at least, socialism.

This last week [1963] I used as meditative material two very strange sources. We have talked about the prayer of meditation and said that normally we use passages from the Gospels—events or words from the life of Christ. But I did not use the Gospels. My first source was a newspaper clipping with a picture of a man named Earl Venay. He is on the list of the ten-most-wanted fugitives in the country. He has made history because, for the first time in fifteen years, two brothers are on the list. I studied the face of this man, who had a most sensitive mouth, eyes which were terribly frightened, and a face filled with pain. I lived with this picture for a part of my time of prayer, trying to face my involvement, trying to live with my guilt.

The second bit of material I used was an article from *The Washington Daily News* about Malcolm X. Four of his brothers were killed by white people; one was hanged. Before Malcolm X was born, while his mother was pregnant with him and at a time when his father was away, the Ku Klux Klan came to his home and broke out the windows. When he was twelve, he was sent to a detention home and later released. He went to a high school where he was the only Negro student and was elected president of his class. His mother became insane and went to a mental institution, where she remains.

A brother of Malcolm X is also in a mental institution. The brother's thinking was so distorted that he was under the delusion that he was Allah, and later on, that he was Allah's superior. Through this brother Malcolm was put in touch with Elijah Muhammed. Elijah Muhammed sent him five dollars and some material on demonology. After he studied this material on demonology, he could never look at the white man in the same light again. I could understand at a new level why it is that Malcolm X and many others feel that the white man is a demon-possessed person of a demon-possessed race.

Not until we can face our own guilt as we look at the society we have perpetuated is there a possibility of actually identifying ourselves as choosing for the outcast. Otherwise we are so guilty that we cannot see. We cannot see the pain in their faces; we are insulated from them. A part of the reason we cannot identify with them is guilt.

Another part of the problem is that most of us have spent our whole lives trying to attain the place where we have certain privileges and advantages. Then we are asked to give up this place if necessary. We have a problem. Middle-class African-Americans also have this problem, but certainly the whites bear by far the greater part of this burden.

I had a talk with a young man from the Lower East Side of New York who had recently become a Christian. He was in Washington with a group that is part of the Young Life Movement. He said that after college he was going back to the Lower East Side to work with the people from whom he had sprung. I asked, "Why are you going back? You have an opportunity to get away from it all."

He replied, "In answer to that, I'll tell you a story. Two men were traveling up a mountain, and one carried a rope and one a brick. When they were close to the top, one said to the other, 'Why are you carrying a rope on this climb?' The other said, 'I'm carrying the rope because if there are others who also would like to reach the top, I shall throw the rope to them and help them up.' Then he said to the first man, 'Why are you carrying the brick?' Said he, 'I'm carrying the brick so I can hurl it at anyone who is also trying to reach the top.'" This illustrates what is so often our attitude of unwillingness to share or to relinquish what we have recently acquired.

The Freedom Movement has identified itself with the outcast and the downtrodden, and the church must make this choice, whatever standing it may lose in the community of the respectable. To be true to its genius and to be a servant people of its Master, the church must, at whatever cost, become involved with, and declare itself to be at the side of the downtrodden, the outcast, and the outlawed.

∾ *Total Commitment* ∾

The degree of commitment is the vital thing—vital to the effectiveness of the mission. An unusual degree of commitment is that which makes the spirit so overwhelming in the Selmas of the South. Such commitment is total, unto death. There are no carefully guarded limits—they have disappeared. Martyrdom has been faced. If martyrdom is a part of the cost, so be it. In a sense, the people who are involved in the Freedom Movement have at certain levels already died. They are not holding on and grasping at life and its privilege, for they have already laid it down. The freedom that comes with this decision is exhilarating.

In contrast, many of us carefully watch the limits of our health and strength. Some of us are very tired. We measure out the love we give to others as from a medicine dropper. But under the baptism of the spirit of Selma, I have seen limits disappear. People walk who cannot walk—the too old, the too young, those with too many responsibilities—are all participating. I am deeply sympathetic with the limits—I understand them—but the power of that spirit which knows no limits is heady stuff.

One of the ways of setting limits and avoiding choosing the outcast is given in the statement sometimes heard, "I am on mission to my family." My response to that is, "Of course you are. It is unthinkable that you not be. You will show concern for others in the setting of your family. You will not neglect wife or child or husband or the legitimate demands of home." There can be, however, a strange selfishness in that claim of devotion to one's family—a way many of us protect ourselves from the outcast and from the real cost of the Gospel.

The demonic structures of society change when one takes on the dispossessed and the dregs of society at the expense of one's personal safety and even, if need be, at the expense of family and loved ones. I saw this more clearly in Selma than ever before. In families there fathers and husbands are working two jobs, not by choice but because of necessity, and mothers are working outside the home. A family, with as many as four, five, or six children, may be carrying three jobs. Domestic help gets ten to twelve dollars a week; if they are well paid, fifteen to sixteen dollars a week. People struggling for survival are the ones who carry on the movement—the ones who are there all night, when there is need to be there all night. They are the ones who are driving three or four times a day in order to pick up the people from Montgomery and bring them back to Selma.

Martin Luther King, Jr., would never say that his first responsibility was to his family. The church of Jesus Christ was never intended to act as chaplain to an individual or to a family. The church is the broken body of Christ laid down for the healing of the broken and the dispossessed and, in this losing of life, family life may be recovered in our time. The totality of this commitment deeply stirs any person who touches the Freedom Movement. In somewhat the same way, a person exploring our community touches lives that are totally committed—people who are willing to face martyrdom for the sake of their mission.

That person then has a choice to make, either to leave or to stay, knowing that his or her life will be irrevocably changed.

∾   *The Church as Corporate Mission*   ∾

The church is not a religious association to strengthen and encourage its members to go out on costly individual mission, although personal, individual missions can be and are vital. The church, the Body of Christ, a servant people includes all of the members, living and dying, young and old. Basic and important in the Christian faith is this corporate dimension of the church, pointing out what society can be, prefiguring life as it will be, a sign of the kingdom to come. We can either like or dislike this fact but, in leaving it at this point, we will have reached no definitive conclusions.

How do we as a people, how does the church of Jesus Christ in the nation's capital, come to embody these principles? How do we become involved with the poor, with the outcast? How do we act with this degree of commitment? How do we do these things corporately?

By the Spirit of God, I believe, a new mission is beginning to emerge in the midst of our people and in the midst of other congregations in our city. For the time being we are calling this a Crusade for the Captive Children. Junior Village is the visible expression of the tragic fruitage of our city's life. Children are paying the price because we have not grappled with the structures of poverty: housing, unemployment, and the hopelessness and hatred which are thus engendered, and in which the children are caught.

Last week I visited Junior Village, where there are almost nine hundred children. Structurally, the village has a capacity of five or six hundred, But that is not the point. A child cannot be given what he needs in an institution. You know how it often is with your own child. At a certain given moment in his life, he needs you for a morning, he needs you for two hours, and he needs you then, not the next day. At Junior Village no one is available to respond to the emotional and spiritual needs of the children.

Although truly dedicated to the work they are doing, the members of the staff have an impossible job, and they are the first ones to tell you that they will never be able to do it. Dedicated volunteers work in a greatly needed program for the preschool children.

The staff also tries to simulate a family situation at mealtimes. However, because of the small number of staff members who are trying to carry out a full schedule for the whole institution, there is simply not enough time. How can you successfully simulate a family mealtime situation only once every several days?

In the hospitals of the city are children who have never left the hospitals—they have not even made it to Junior Village. They do not know how to smile because they have had no one to smile at them. In years past articles have been published, editorials have been written, the conscience of the city has been somewhat aroused, but the years go by and the children are still there. In such conditions Malcolm Xs are being bred and Earl Venays are being created. They are there, and we let them stay there.

In a city like Washington, certainly one thousand foster homes could be found. Or, if each of the eight hundred or more churches in this metropolitan area would sponsor one child, all the children could be released from Junior Village and perhaps many of them could be restored to their own families.

The members of the new mission that is emerging feel that this is really possible, that we can give these children love, we can give them homes, we can turn them around, we can give each of them a face and an identity. We thought perhaps we might take pictures of these children as a way of introducing them to potential families, but we learned that you may not take a picture of the face of a child in Junior Village. You may take a picture only of the back of the head!

Well, let's take the back of her head and then let's turn her around. Let's find her a home. The aim of the mission is to free the children within a year. If we have not done it before then, let's have M-Day when every child is released from Junior Village. Let's enlist all of the churches of the city, all the agencies of the city, every concerned person—let's start at this point. We must start with something challeng-ing. Why should the church always come in with too little too late, simply joining an effort someone else has started at the grassroots level? Why don't we start at the grassroots level and then let others come in? Let's do it as a total Body of Christ. [For Love of Children (FLOC), formed in response to this call, led the campaign to demon-strate alternatives superior to having an institution for the care of dependent children. Junior Village was closed in 1973.]

With this effort as just the beginning, let us go on to other things: Home Rule, cleaning out the slums, whatever needs to be done. We will need the young, and we will need the old. We will need people to write, and we will need people to interpret. We will need people to tramp the pavements, to seek out the homes of potential foster parents. We will need people to demonstrate the need for legislation and to work for the enactment of just laws.

Jesus came in order that the oppressed might go free, the captives might be released, and the blind might see. We can seriously tackle the structures of poverty, and keep on until the day is done and the shadows flee away and the busy world is hushed, and our work is finished. And whatever is needed, we believe God will provide.

Listen, and learn whether there is a call here for you.

Notes

[1] Dietrich Bonhoeffer, *Letters and Papers from Prison*, ed. Eberhard Bethge (New York: Macmillan, 1953), p. 361.

[2] Albert H. Van den Heuvel, *The Humiliation of the Church* (Louisville, Ky.: Westminster/John Knox Press, 1966), p. 56.

[3] Bonhoeffer, *Letters and Papers from Prison*, p. 361.

21

How Much Is Enough?

~

This call for responsible and responsive stewardship was presented in 1990.

The Ministry of Money holds a workshop dealing with the fascinating question: How much is enough? Since this is a very basic question for everyone and, although I will say in advance that I have no answers, I believe that we grow by carefully considering and living with the right questions.

In 2 Corinthians 8, Paul writes about taking up an offering for the home church in Jerusalem. He was seeking to equalize the pressures on the churches, since the Jerusalem congregation was poorer than those that had been newly established. Beginning with verse 12, Paul says that, provided there is an eager desire to give, God accepts what a person has and does not ask for what a person has not. There is no question of relieving others at the cost of hardship to ourselves; it is a question of equality. At the moment our surplus meets their need. But one day our need may be met from their surplus. The aim is equality. As Scripture has it, the person who received much had no more than enough, and the one who received little did not go short.

A second pertinent passage is from the book of Acts, chapter 3, beginning with verse 1.

> One day at three in the afternoon, the hour of prayer, Peter and John were on their way up to the temple. Now a man who had been a cripple from birth used to be carried there and laid every day by the gate of the temple called "Beautiful Gate," to beg from people as they went in. [We are certainly more accustomed now to seeing beggars than we used to be. We pass

them every day on the streets of our city.] When he saw Peter
and John on their way into the temple he asked for charity.
["Can you spare a quarter?"] But Peter fixed his eyes on him, as
John did also, and said, "Look at us." Expecting a gift from
them, the man was all attention. And Peter said, "I have no
silver or gold; but what I have I give you: in the name of Jesus
Christ of Nazareth, walk." Then he grasped him by the right
hand and pulled him up; and at once his feet and ankles grew
strong; he sprang up, stood on his feet, and started to walk. He
entered the temple with them, leaping and praising God as he
went. Everyone saw him walking and praising God, and when
they recognized him as the man who used to sit begging at
Beautiful Gate, they were filled with wonder and amazement at
what had happened to him.

And as he was clutching Peter and John all the people came
running in astonishment towards them in Solomon's Portico, as
it is called. Peter saw them coming and met them with these
words: "Men of Israel, why be surprised at this? Why stare at us
as if we had made this man walk by some power or godliness of
our own? The God of Abraham, Isaac, and Jacob, the God of
our fathers, has given the highest honour to his servant Jesus,
whom you committed for trial and repudiated in Pilate's court—
repudiated the one who was holy and righteous when Pilate had
decided to release him. You begged as a favour the release of a
murderer, and killed him who has led the way to life. But God
raised him from the dead; of that we are witnesses. And the
name of Jesus, by awakening faith, has strengthened this man,
whom you see and know, and this faith has made him completely well, as you can all see for yourselves." (Acts 3:1–16)

The question for all of us is how much shall we have? What is appropriate, considering who we say we are? The world consists of many
people who are satiated, and an increasing number who live in what
Brueggemann calls dehumanizing, despairing, demeaning scarcity. In
light of this condition, well-known to us, how much should I have? What
is enough for me? What should you have? What is enough for you?

Not to ask the question is to live in massive unconsciousness. Let's
remind ourselves of the context in which we ask this basic question.
First, we ask the question within the framework of church. We are the
called people of God. Brueggemann says, "Church is where God's
glory is manifest in an earthly community of grace." Churches are
people incarnating God's nature; God is love, righteousness, compassion. To see the real church is to see God's face—to see an incarnation
in time and space of God's very being.

The church is an alternative culture, over and against the standards of the world. In general, the church has been infiltrated by the value systems of the world, and the sadness is that we fail to recognize the infiltration. We moderate and polish off the world's thinking, and name it Christian. The church embodies the upside-down kingdom. Whatever the world admires is probably not good, according to kingdom values. The church is always anti-empire.

The question of how much is enough will most likely be answered differently by bankers in the trust departments of our banks (or even by ordinary persons on the street, because there is not that much difference in their value systems). The question would be answered quite differently by one who is seriously following Jesus. We are asking the question from within the Body of the crucified, risen Jesus. In this context, how much is enough?

The larger context is the culture in which we, the church, are living, and it is the only period of history in which we will live. We know that every period has its special difficulties. But our period in time is radically different from any period in which people have lived before.

Brueggemann says that we are living in the time of brinkmanship. He says the church must face the fact that we live in a culture that is in serious trouble and that the time is short for conducting business as usual. Our economic institutions and habits are dysfunctional and seem to be disintegrating. But, along with these facts, the more immediate concern for us is that the vision of humanness and humaneness we so treasure in the Gospel is being forgotten. These values are not found even within the Body of Christ. "We are at the very brink of our common destruction; reordering a common economy may be a modest step against such brinkmanship."

Because of our economy, its presuppositions, and our heightening consumer mentality, we are on the brink of losing the home that God has given us. We rightly deplore homelessness, and our community works with this problem in some depth. To have no home is to be utterly miserable, but one at least has the earth to sleep on and air to breathe. We are, however, coming to the point where nature will no longer be able to support our addiction to satiation.

Matthew Fox begins his book *The Coming of the Cosmic Christ* with a dream that he had on March 15, 1988, at the Kirkridge Retreat Center in Pennsylvania. He woke up and the dream was very,

very vivid in his mind. The essence of it was "Your mother Is dying."
He broke down that dream in the first part of his book into these
sections: "Mother Earth Is Dying," "The Mystical Brain Is Dying,"
"Creativity Is Dying," "Wisdom Is Dying," "The Youth Are Dying,"
"Native People, Their Religions, and Cultures Are Dying," "Mother
Church Is Dying," "Mother Love, Compassion Is Dying." It's matri-
cide at the hands of those who are the patriarchs and those who have
violated the whole maternal dimension of our lives. The last section of
this first part is, "Our Mother Is Dying, But Not Dead."[1] Therein lies
the hope. But unless the dying dimension is understood, there is no
hope.

Thomas Berry in *The Dream of the Earth* says:

> The difficulty comes when the industrial mode of our economy
> disrupts the natural processes, when human technologies
> become destructive of earth's technologies. In such a situation
> the productivity of the natural world and its life systems is
> diminished. When nature goes into deficit, then we go into
> deficit.
>   When this occurs to a limited extent on a regional basis, it can
> often be remedied. The difficulty is when the entire planetary
> system is affected. The earth system is most threatened when
> the human economy goes out of balance and frantic efforts
> toward a remedy lead to a reckless plundering of the land,
> spending our capital as our interest diminishes.[2]

Berry says that the specific data available on the U.S. economy
indicates that

> we now have a gross national product of more than $4 trillion.
> [A billion is a thousand million, and a trillion is a thousand
> billion. Just work with that a bit—4 trillion dollars!] In the year
> 1987, we also had a national debt of more than $2 trillion, an
> annual budgetary deficit of some $150 billion, an infrastructure
> disintegration requiring repairs of $750 billion.[3]

Looked at from a personal point of view, this would be a time when
your house begins to deteriorate but you put off making the repairs.
For the nation, the necessary repairs have to do with highways,
bridges, sewage systems. Our whole infrastructure system in this
country needs $750 billion a year.

> [We have] a trade deficit of more than $150 billion. Third World
> financial loans unlikely to be repaid of more than $200 billion,
> and annual military expenditures of $300 billion.[4]

All of these can be considered financial deficits leading eventually to
what Berry calls "earth deficits." Such deficits result in the closing down
of the basic life system of the planet through the abuse of the air, the
soil, the water, and the vegetation.

The *Washington Post* reported information about the *Exxon
Valdez* oil spill [March 24, 1989] and what it cost in terms of the
environment: 36,471 dead birds, 1,016 dead otters, 144 bald eagles,
the salmon spawning patterns interrupted for decades. Dan Rather
spoke about twelve similar major oil spills this last year, one of which
spilled 75,000 tons of oil, twice as much as that spilled in Alaska. The
rivers are dying. The oceans are dying. And this is the home that we
have been given.

These deficits cause not only irreparable loss of resources, but the
death of the living process. And not simply the death of a living process
but of *the* living process, a living process which exists, so far as we
know, only on the planet earth. Our problem is definitively different
from the problems of other generations of whatever ethnic, cultural,
political, or religious tradition or historical period. For the first time we
are determining the destiny of the earth in a comprehensive and
irreversible manner. The immediate danger is not possible nuclear war
but industrial plundering. Berry says,

> We are indeed closing down the major life systems of the
> planet. . . . We are changing the chemistry of the planet. We
> are altering the great hydrological cycles. We are weakening the
> ozone layer which shields us from cosmic rays. We are saturat-
> ing the air, the water, and the soil with toxic substances so that
> we can never bring them back to their original purity. We are
> upsetting the entire earth system that has, over some billions of
> years and through an endless sequence of experiments, produced
> such a magnificent array of living forms, forms capable of
> seasonal self-renewal over an indefinite period of time.[5]

In the past, one species has been eliminated every two thousand years.
Now one is eliminated every twenty-five minutes.

We are playing brinkmanship. Our mother is dying. We, even the
Christian church, are not acting as though we are on the brink. Against

this backdrop we as the church ask the question, "How much is enough?"

What do we need, really need? I don't know, for you—or for me. But it is important to raise the question often. First of all, we need to consider the question of our needs against an understanding of what the planet can sustain without throwing it into deficit. We know that the planet cannot sustain our present level of satiation. All the people in the world cannot possibly live as we live in the United States. It cannot be done. Even a tiny section of the world cannot live much longer as we live. The planet simply cannot sustain our present level of satiation.

Our level has been sustained by industrial plundering and our addictive consumerism. So we need to ask what level can be sustained for all of us on the planet—not just for the United States and a few favored nations, but for all the family of God.

As for the principle of equality which Paul set forth in the first chapter of 2 Corinthians, the determination of our need must be seen through the principle of equalization—and surely equalization with those of our own community of faith.

In the community of faith known as the Jubilee Church, one member earns approximately $7,500 a year. She gets up about 4:00 A.M., to go to work in the cold and darkness of the winter. She has several children and an aunt in Sierra Leone. One of the children cannot find work, and they all suffer from lack of food and other necessities of life. Other members of Jubilee Church have an income of more than ten times as much. What does the principle of equalization mean under those circumstances?

I have a need for leisure; I have a need to eat in a restaurant; I have a need for a break in my schedule because of the pressure; and on and on it goes. But what if I am in the same community with that person who earns $7,500 a year?

This principle of equalization presents a problem to be solved not only for the people in my faith community but for all the marginal people in the world. This became very clear to me last week when a person walked ten or twelve feet into the Potter's House [a Christian coffee house operated by The Church of the Saviour] and collapsed. He was far from being an aesthetic, sanitary creature so several of us got up and, as gently as we could, pulled him outside and tried to decide what we should do. Had he passed out just temporarily? Should we call an ambulance? After we had spent some time with him, we learned that he had active TB and AIDS and was dying. I looked at him and said to myself, "What about this principle of equalization? If it doesn't mean something here, there's certainly no use talking about it on a Sunday morning. What does it mean? This is my brother!"

What about the woman who lives day and night in the nearby little park, sleeps right there on the corner? She's a half-block away. What about her? And what about all of the other people in the world? What sort of connections do I have? How do I live? How much is enough for me when these persons are a part of the human family, the Body of Christ? Equalization!

To me it is obvious that we should reduce our physical security needs and transmute those needs to deeper needs: the need for silence, the need for love, the need for friendship, and the need for serving others. Many of us feel that our needs are not being met. Maybe they are not our real needs, the real needs of our deepest being. Maybe they are demands being made on life.

What changes our perception of need? Why do some people with very little in the way of material things, and very little or no family security, feel deeply blessed and overwhelmed by life's bounty? Why are they under a constant barrage of grace, bombarded by goodness?

The clearest illustration I know of is Brother Francis. He is a social worker with Samaritan Inns. I never run across him when he's not in great shape, thanking God for all of the goodness of life! For the first few months that I knew him, I was certain that that attitude of his couldn't last. It just couldn't be real! He's a monk, wandering around right in the middle of all this need. Yet he never has the feeling he's overworked or has too much to do. He's a joy! He doesn't have anything, and certainly does not have all his financial future worked out. Every time we pray together his prayer is always one of thanksgiving, just for the joy of being able to be there. Some of us have pushed him pretty hard, life has pushed him pretty hard—but we haven't found a crack yet. Things are genuine with Brother Francis! He is bombarded by grace, bombarded by goodness.

I believe an attitude like that of Brother Francis has to do with connectedness in three areas of life. Our needs change depending upon our degree of connectedness in these three areas:

First, our connectedness to God. A deep connection must come before what Matthew Fox calls, "the recovery of the mystical consciousness." We don't have just an idea of God—we are really connected. To the degree we are connected with or are related to a beneficent, manna-producing God, we do not have to provide for our own private surplus. If we know the manna will be there as we need it, we won't have to rent a storage bin to hold the extra stuff. To be connected with God is to trust the flow. The flow is infinite—it will never run out. Jesus said, "Do not be anxious. . . . Consider the lilies of the field, how they grow" (Matt. 6:25–28, *RSV*). Relax into God's infinite bounty—you will be taken care of. Paul says, "What have you that you did not receive?" (1 Cor. 4:7, *RSV*). We can add, "What will you need in the future that you will not receive?" God is a giving God and will bountifully supply all our needs. So deepen your connectedness with the unseen, real realm beyond this world. "You shall love the Lord your God with all your heart, and with all your soul, and with all your mind" (Matt. 22:37, *RSV*)—that is the great commandment. As we deepen our mystical consciousness we begin to live in that unseen realm. Amazing how little we need when we're connected.

The second area: your needs will change as you deepen your connectedness with people. By nature, by essence, we co-inhere with one another. We are not isolated individuals; we are members of one another, of all others. To the degree that I sense the connectedness, I do not want to be relieved of pressures that others have to live with. I do not want security that others lack. To the degree that I sense myself really connected, I want equality. Just as I would want it in a human family, I want equality even more deeply in the larger family of faith and the whole human family. I want to give what before I thought I needed to hold on to for my own and my loved ones' safety. Now I know that I cannot protect myself or my loved ones. I need to give to another's need, and that need is deeper than my own need to possess. As our connections with one another deepen, our personal needs decrease. We become much freer with our time and our money.

Wouldn't it be a tremendously lubricating thing if we could be free to give money to those experiencing scarcity? We run across them all the time. We tell these people, "I will pray for you," but very seldom do we say, "You need money, I'll give you money." So money is much more sacred to us than prayer. We have trouble giving money, and people have trouble receiving it. Money should be flowing all over the place, because we are giving to those who are experiencing scarcity at the moment.

This connectedness needs to include everyone with whom we come in contact. We will not be uneasy with the homeless beggar in the street, that woman lying in the park a half-block away. She's my sister; she belongs to me and I to her. Why should I be uneasy with her when I believe in the principle of equality?

The third area of connectedness is connectedness to the planet, to the universe. In this area we have become pathological. We have separated ourselves from our planet, and this is suicidal. Thomas Berry again:

> Every being has its own interior, its self, its mystery, its numinous aspect. To deprive any being of this sacred quality is to disrupt the larger order of the universe. Reverence will be total or it will not be at all. The universe does not come to us in pieces any more than a human individual stands before us with some part of its being.
>
> Preservation of this feeling for reality in its depths has been considerably upset in these past two centuries of scientific analysis and technological manipulation of the earth and its energies. During this period, the human mind lived in the narrowest bonds that it ever experienced. The vast mythic, visionary, symbolic world with its all-pervasive, numinous qualities was lost. Because of this loss, we made our terrifying assault upon the earth with an irrationality that is stunning in enormity, while we were being assured that this was the way to a better, more humane, more reasonable world.[6]

We lost that sense of connection with our human habitat. Our Native American forebears sensed the numinous quality of the earth. Many people still sense it. Chief Seattle said in 1854:

> Every part of this country is sacred to my people. Every glittering pine needle, every sandy beach, all the mists in the dark forests, the rocky hills, the gentle meadows, the bodily warmth of ponies and of people—they all belong to the same family.

As I deepen my connectedness with my natural habitat I don't want to assault it any longer. Whatever the personal cost, I want to live in natural harmony with it. I want to give to it, and I want to draw from its wisdom, its beauty, and its grandeur. This is the attitude we need to acquire as we work with the question, How much is enough? Brueggemann points out that in Acts 5, when Ananias and Sapphira were holding back from the common good, from the community, the issue for them was one of death. They were trying to build up a private surplus. In Acts 3 Peter and John had nothing to give, no silver or gold, but they had the power of healing. Those of us who have so much probably do not have the power of healing, which is a prime purpose of the church.

I have said that I don't know what I should have, and you probably don't know what you should have. But I think one of the most powerful things we can do for one another is to tell our stories. "This is what I have; this is what I give away; this is what I feel is right for me at this moment. But let me really tell you in detail." If we start telling these stories to one another, and if we listen to the stories, I believe healing will take place, and we will be given insight as to what is appropriate and what is right.

We tried telling our stories at a recent evening session of the Ministry of Money. After I had spoken and thought about what I had said, I wondered whether I had just polished up the whole secular conception of what it's all about, and whether I had really penetrated this upside-down kingdom at all. I knew, however, that it surely does help to tell the story—in detail. And to let others hear it and consider it even when it makes you feel queasy and uneasy.

Seriously dealing with the questions—How much is enough? How can we meet the need to equalize?—is, I firmly believe, our hope for salvation.

Notes

[1] Matthew Fox, *The Coming of the Cosmic Christ* (San Francisco: Harper & Row, 1988), p. 13.

[2] Thomas Berry, *The Dream of the Earth* (San Francisco: Sierra Club Books, 1988), p. 71.

[3] Ibid., pp. 71–72.

[4] Ibid.

[5] Ibid., p. 206.

[6] Ibid., pp. 134–35.

Part VII

~⁓~

Old Battles, New Challenges

22

D-Day—Then and Now

~

This reflection was written in 1994, the fiftieth anniversary of the Invasion of Normandy.

God often speaks to me through what others think it might be helpful for me to do. During the last couple of weeks, when so much of the Western World's attention has been focused on the Normandy Invasion fifty years ago, a number of people have said, "Talk to us about that period in your life. You were on Omaha Beach on D-Day. Our history as a church is linked with your history in those days. What did that experience do to you? How did it shape you and your sense of call in which we have shared? We really want to know."

I have resisted these requests for many reasons that seemed legitimate to me. But last Monday was D-Day plus fifty years. Next Sunday is our members' congregational meeting. In this particular period following D-Day fifty years ago, many necessary things crystallized within me that have found expression in our lives together in the community we call The Church of the Saviour.

Next Sunday we will dialogue vigorously around deep issues which will affect the future of our people for years to come. So perhaps several of these seminal experiences may be helpful to share, though they are very personal, and some of them are a part of the record that Elizabeth O'Connor has chronicled for us.

First, let me say a word about belief—faith. Much of our real power for Christ and the kingdom comes from the depths of our belief and faith. When the father of the epileptic son asks Jesus if it is possible to help him, Jesus responds: "If it is possible! . . . Everything is possible to one who has faith" (Mark 9:23). In Matthew 17 Jesus says, "Your faith is too small." He affirms, "If you have faith no bigger even than a mustard-seed, you will say to this mountain, 'Move from here to there!' and it will move; nothing will prove impossible for you" (Matt. 17:20).

As a chaplain, my sole task was to share faith, nurture faith, deepen faith—in men under extreme conditions of crisis. Men who, after I met them, often had only a few hours or days or weeks to live.

In each of the three major engagements of our division, we lost by death or serious wounding 50 percent of our division. We suffered a 150 percent loss in eight months. You, of course, cannot have casualties of 150 percent without constant replacement. You can imagine the intensity of that scene.

My task in that context was clear: to share faith and belief—not personally to survive. My conviction is that that is really the task and context for all of us who love Jesus. Jesus asks, "Do you love me?" If the answer is yes, then "feed my sheep." Our task is to share belief, to nurture belief, to deepen belief.

The context for everyone in today's world is much more dramatic than we realize. People are homeless and dying on our streets. There are victims of AIDS. (Ask Janelle and Allen Goetcheus the number of funerals they have attended in the last few years.) Tens of thousands of people in our city are economically helpless, refugees from other nations, with no jobs, children being shaped by a hostile, violent culture of disbelief. Society is being managed by triage. We, the privileged, will win. You can perish; you are not needed.

Talk about warfare! We are storming the beaches now. I see our present context in Washington as dramatic and much more demanding than that dramatic period when we wondered whether we would be driven back into the sea. My task on the beach was the sharing, nurturing, and deepening of faith for those about to perish. Our task now on our current beach is the same: strengthening of belief.

How are we doing on this beachhead in our broken, bleeding city? Of course, we share beliefs at whatever level we believe. We cannot give away that which has not been given to us. We exude into others belief at whatever level we have it at the moment. If another needs belief desperately at the moment and we do not have it, that opportunity is missed.

The thing I am most grateful for from my experience in Normandy is the deepening of my belief. I worked in a new way with the question of whether I really had faith in the traditional beliefs I had assumed all my conscious life, and whether I would let my full weight down on God— the spiritual realm of God—and spend the rest of my life getting detached from everything else.

There were several important formative experiences in this new deepening of belief.

A few days after the breakthrough from the beach itself, the command came through to destroy an enemy stronghold on a low-lying ridge in front of us. It was well fortified. Our attack was to begin about 2:00 A.M. We were to take the ridge, whatever it cost in casualties. I had to determine how to be faithful to my work in the several hours before 2:00 A.M. I decided to make as many "pastoral visits" as possible. These visits, of necessity, would be in the foxholes of the men. That meant fairly close quarters.

I dropped into the hole of a man I had never seen before and said, "I'm your chaplain. Thought maybe you would like to talk."

"Chaplain, I'm glad you're here. I have a clear, intuitive feeling that I'm going to die tonight. I don't know God. Talk to me about God. Don't give me the usual stuff. If there is a God, I'll be meeting that God within four hours. Perhaps sooner. Start talking."

That provided a reality check for me. God would look at my work as a chaplain within four hours. It felt a little different than filling in my periodic chaplain's report, which was sent to the chief of chaplain's office to be evaluated.

I checked the casualty reports the following day. That sheep of mine had died that night. Had he been "fed"? Had belief been given?

A few days later I was called upon to perform a funeral service for a friend who had been killed several days earlier, whose body had become very bloated. The formerly handsome face was discolored and swollen and unrecognizable. His shroud was a discarded parachute.

In the preceding months that we had been together and become friends, he was the one person physically present who understood my deepest questions and longings. When I shared my earliest intimations about a new kind of church, which was to become The Church of the Saviour, he said, "If I live, I'll move to Washington and help you start the church you describe." It's marvelous to have at least one such spiritual companion at each phase of one's journey.

I looked down at my dead, disfigured friend. It was raining. My alcoholic jeep driver was trying to stand up beside me. Ominous sounding artillery fire was not far away. From my wet New Testament I was trying to read:

> If there be no resurrection, then Christ was not raised; and if Christ was not raised, then our Gospel is null and void, and so is your faith; and we turn out to be lying witnesses for God. . . . If it is for this life only that Christ has given us hope, we of all men are most to be pitied." (1 Cor. 15:13–19)

I cannot ever remember feeling more alone and hopeless. It was a pathetic scene. I can feel it now.

Then, for me, there was a Presence. The spiritual world was all around us and in me. I had to work with new feelings: envy and longing. I could feel and sense the resurrection aliveness of my friend. I was in touch with that Beyond world. I felt sorry for myself for having been left behind. Now all the surrounding ethos felt different. Contending armies were pathetic and feeble in the light of this surrounding, penetrating reality. I now knew, believed experientially, that which I before would have said I believed. But the level of belief had changed. I had struck rock, "Rock of Ages, cleft for me [for us]. Let me hide myself in Thee." At a deeper level than any before, everything was solid.

I have often recalled that reality at countless later funerals. Death became different each time that flashback returned.

A few days later there was a lull in the fighting. The time came to gather in the dead. I volunteered to be with a small group picking up dead bodies scattered through the hedgerows and fields alongside the bodies of decaying cattle. The cows and the men had often died together. I would look at the faces of the men. Some I knew; many I didn't. All were so young.

When we finished our work that day there must have been five hundred bodies piled up like cordwood. Soon after, I began the work of writing to as many of these men's families as I could.

It was about this period that I began to notice men breaking under the strain of it all. One young, formerly macho man came to me. He said, "It's all over for me. This morning while I was trying to shoot a man, my rifle turned into a writhing serpent. It was impossible to aim it. It was impossible to fire it. Now it is a living writhing thing in my hands. Can you help me? I'll be court-martialed for defection, but I can't keep on."

Then I began to notice another phenomenon. As I talked to a man, in the midst of a good conversation his eyes would glaze over and a few seconds later the person I had been talking to was gone. He had taken all he could hear, and he was escaping into an inner world. The war for him was over for a time. For some, when this happened, it was for the duration.

This became my milieu. My old world had crumbled. None of my old certainties existed. My question became this: Does the faith that sustained me in childhood and in my early youth hold under these chaotic and cruel conditions?

This question was not only for that time. It is the question for us now. The world we knew a few years ago is in ruins. Can we, do we believe? "If you have faith no bigger even than a mustard-seed . . . " (Matt. 17:20).

The pressure in Normandy—the pressure now—does not of itself produce faith. There is an expression, "There are no atheists in foxholes." I know, however, that there are many fatalists in foxholes, many fearful people in foxholes, many cynics in foxholes. And many are holding their options open.

Under intense pressure people can glaze over and burn out. They survive on a surface level. Many become cynical. "This is a horrible world. I'll take from it everything I can." Many veterans are not finer people for their experiences.

Because of the intensity and the starkness of human need, we can hear God's question—Jesus' question—"Do you believe? Do you love me? Will you take the leap? Will you leap into my arms? Will you come home? Will you leave the way of security, power, violence, force, killing, triage? Will you, with me, see a new city—a new nation, a new church? Won't you believe there is everything beyond? Won't you believe the resurrection is the ultimate reality? Will you hear my call to commitment?" This is the commitment I tried to make during those days fifty years ago.

Under difficult circumstances now, I believe we must make that commitment by faith, by believing. Jesus says, "Your faith is too small." This commitment to belong to Jesus in this other resurrection realm is not just personal. At a board meeting of Samaritan Inns last week, Killian Noe gave us the image of a mother whose house is on fire with the children inside. She has a mandate to go in. It's not optional; it's not rational. She goes in just because of who she is.

Like the mother in Killian's story, we must do what the current crisis requires. For us, as for Moses, the waters will part.